THE **NATURAL FOODS** *COOKBOOK*

A wealth of flavourful dishes which are quick and easy to prepare, plus lots of help in planning energy-packed menus to keep you fit and well.

GW00598928

By the same author:
THE WHOLEGRAIN RECIPE BOOK

THE NATURAL FOODS COOKBOOK

Eat your way to better health

by

Marlis Weber

Translated from the German by Amanda Pask

Line illustrations by Paul Davies

THORSONS PUBLISHERS LIMITED
Wellingborough, Northamptonshire

First published in Germany as *Natürkuche gesund & lecker* (1982)

© Walter Hadecke Verlag, 7252 Weil der Stadt, Lukas-Moser-Weg 2, West Germany

First published in the United Kingdom 1985

© THORSONS PUBLISHERS LIMITED 1985

British Library Cataloguing in Publication Data

Weber, Marlis
  The natural foods cookbook.
  1. Cookery (Natural foods)
  I. Title   II. Naturküche gesund & lecker,
  English
  641.5'637   TX741

  ISBN 0-7225-0886-7

Printed and bound in Great Britain

CONTENTS

		Page
Foreword		7
Introduction		9
Chapter		
1.	Breakfasts	25
2.	Soups, Starters and Snacks	31
3.	Main Dishes	46
4.	Vegetable Dishes	67
5.	Salads	98
6.	Sauces and Dressings	118
7.	Desserts	123
8.	Breads, Cakes and Pastries	134
9.	Drinks	144
	Appendix: Diet Guidelines	151
	Index	157

FOREWORD

These days, nutrition — eating a well-balanced diet — should be the concern of everyone, for whoever overlooks this runs the risk of damaging his health or suffering one of the diet-related illnesses which are now so widespread.

In the last century it was still possible and relatively easy to make sure of a good diet. For one thing most people at that time used muscle power at work, thereby burning up significant amounts of calorific energy. On the other hand, refined foods were still not generally available, and most were therefore natural wholefoods.

Today, being overweight has become a problem through sedentary occupations, lack of exercise, the temptations of refined food products and the sheer amount of food and drink consumed. In cases of overweight there is a tendency to develop diet-related disorders, in particular diabetes, gout, arthritis, heart disease and arteriosclerosis, liver and gall-bladder troubles.

Seductive advertising campaigns, which skilfully encourage the consumer to spend excessive amounts on unhealthy food products, make it even more difficult to maintain a balanced approach when it comes to nutrition, and it is little wonder that so many people are taken in by such tactics.

Nevertheless, proper nutrition is something which can be learnt — just like reading, writing, sewing or driving. Willpower is all that is required, together with a commitment to giving up bad eating habits. It also helps to understand the principles of good nutrition and know how to apply them. Progress in the field of science has led to a greater understanding of biochemical processes in the human body; for example, it is recognized that in cases of relatively small energy requirements, sugar and insulin are pumped into the blood after every sweet meal or snack, resulting in the conversion of sugar to fat and the build up of fatty deposits. It is undoubtedly for this reason that many of our contemporaries are too fat.

'Not too much, not too sweet and not too fatty'

This is now the most significant rule concerning good nutrition. It is easily remembered and not hard to follow either. Incidentally, gourmets need not fear that this will spoil their enjoyment of good food. The main thing is to select from the great stream of food products on offer just those which are natural and contain the most nutrients. For correct nourishment a food's 'health value' is seen in terms of its natural vitamin, mineral and fibre content which contributes to the maintenance of good health.

In today's circumstances the foods which are of least value to us are those containing concentrated energy whilst lacking all vitamins, trace elements, essential proteins and linoleic acid or other biologically vital substances. Primarily this group of foods includes refined sugar, starch flours, refined flours and cooking fats, as well as all products made with them. If one eats these 'denatured' foods in large quantities, the intake of calories soars whilst the supply of nutrients which maintains the 'living structure' and functions of the body is neglected. It is quite possible to be under-nourished by any amount of food if the health-giving substances already mentioned are not present.

Those foods with the greatest protective value in terms of our health are without doubt raw vegetables, fruit, wholegrains and their products, particularly brown rice, millet, fresh milk, Quark, and natural vegetable oils. Cereals represent, to some extent, a natural and tightly packed store of numerous vital nutrients, and it is therefore an ideal food for daily consumption in the form of flakes or a porridge as a breakfast dish. This will also ensure an adequate intake of fibre, well recognized as an important food for the smooth functioning of the intestines.

The most difficult thing is to learn how to balance the intake of protein, fat and carbohydrates so that they have a favourable effect on the body's biochemical activities and prevent overweight, even when there is a lack of exercise and only slight energy requirements. In such cases, the aim is to avoid too much carbohydrate and fat and slightly increase the intake of protein. But whoever wants to make himself really familiar with this basic idea needs to have some knowledge of food composition and the number of calories and joules and amounts of carbohydrate, protein and fat each food contains.

However, this book does not aim to be a comprehensive manual on nutrition. The author has concentrated on improving the quality of nutrition by way of numerous helpful hints, picked up through experience, technical culinary information and good recipes.

Marlis Weber relies on the use of simple wholefoods, her preparation of which is designed to preserve their health-giving properties as far as possible. She also bases many of her recipes on protein form sources other than meat — for example: milk, Quark, cheese, eggs and vegetables.

As a dietitian and a doctor, I am naturally concerned that the ideas of nutrition 'counselling' should reflect modern scientific developments in this field. All too often, books are published which convey a one-sided or extreme dietary principle, and thereby confuse their readers.

The author is a dietitian, is experienced in lecturing on the subject of wholefood nutrition and has worked with me for many years. Her accomplishments are a sign of her practical experience and knowledge of this subject and her ability to convey this understanding to her reader.

DR HELMUT ANEMULLER

INTRODUCTION

Eating Naturally: A Pleasure

Healthy, natural eating is very important, but some of the most common objections to it are lengthy preparation of foods, expense, difficulty in learning the basic principles of a healthy diet, and a lack of flavour. These are the prejudiced and often deeply ingrained opinions of people who have never looked too closely at the subject of nutrition. In contrast, I have seen how fast such an interest can be developed if wholefoods are first explained and demonstrated at classes.

This book aims at breaking down such prejudices and proving that a healthy meal with nourishing food need not be time-consuming or expensive; neither is it difficult to learn the basic idea of wholefood cooking, and, above all, it can taste excellent.

Meat and fish recipes have purposely been left out, mostly since the average consumption of these foods is too high and can result in an excessive intake of fat, cholesterol, purine and preservatives. I shall try to show that an ovolactovegetarian diet with eggs, milk, wholegrain cereals and cereal products, fruit, vegetables, nuts, seeds, high-grade vegetable oils and fats can be full of variety and value. The most important thing is to cut down on the use of refined products and to eat more foods with a high 'health-value' — those with a high proportion of vital nutrients, a low proportion (or no!) harmful additives, which are wholesome and left in their natural state.

Why Healthy Eating is so Important

It is certainly a sorry state of affairs that amongst the countries of the world there is on the one hand, an excess of food (with about 40 per cent of the population being overweight), and on the other hand, there is a striking shortage of food in many areas. Nutritional reports drawn up on Western societies show quite clearly how questionable the dietary habits of many people are:

★ On average too many calories are consumed; more food is eaten than is necessary.
★ On average too many fatty foods are present in the diet; they make up to 40 per cent of the calorific intake, whereas 30-35 per cent would do.
★ Most people eat too many sweet foods; 4 oz (100g) of refined sugar per day!
★ Most people also eat too much salt; twice as much sodium is used as is necessary.
★ In addition most people drink too much alcohol; it makes up about 6 per cent of the total calorific intake.

These are all contributory factors in the development of diet-induced illnesses, such as tooth decay, diabetes, gout and arthritis, heart and circulatory disorders and many others. It is also worth considering that a wrong choice of ingredients and cooking methods can affect the quantity of essential nutrients in your food; by 'essential nutrients' is meant vitamin B_1, vitamin B_2, folic acid, vitamin B_6, calcium, iron (for women) and iodine (according to where you live).

Proper nutrition should provide the body with all the substances it needs in the correct quantities; this will ensure normal body weight, activity, health and enjoyment of life.

The Basic Principles of a Wholefood Diet

1. The calorific intake should be suited to the requirements of the individual.
2. Proportions of carbohydrate, fat and protein in the diet should be controlled:
   approx. 50-55 per cent carbohydrates;
   approx. 35 per cent fats;
   approx. 10-15 per cent protein.
3. 'Essential' nutrients (i.e., those which the body needs but cannot synthesize itself), such as vitamins, minerals, trace elements, essential fatty acids and certain elements of protein, should be ensured in the diet. The best way to do this is to include foods which contain balanced proportions of natural essential nutrients and energy-giving ingredients.
4. Wholefoods (i.e., foods in their natural state) are best, and also ensure an adequate intake of as yet unidentified nutrients.
5. The daily intake of food should be divided into five or six separate mealtimes.

Simple Rules for Wholefood Cooking

★ Have breakfast in peace (if at all possible), and eat plenty. Muesli, porridge, Quark and fruit, or wholewheat bread, low-fat cheese, egg or vegetarian pâté are just a few ideas for suitable choices. Also have a drink of herbal tea, milk or fruit juice.
★ Small snacks between meals are important — usually a drink of fruit or vegetable juice, milk or buttermilk with a savoury crispbread or piece of home-made cake will be enough; or simply have a piece of fresh fruit or a raw vegetable to nibble.
★ Main meals should always include a salad or raw fruit. Quark, cheese or soya products are good providers of protein and do not contain too much fat which should be avoided.
★ For salad dressings use high-grade, cold-pressed vegetable oils. For spreading and cooking use only butter or soft vegetable margarines.
★ Sugar should be used sparingly and is best avoided altogether. Instead, make full use of

small quantities of naturally sweet ingredients such as honey, pear or apple concentrates, fruit sugar and dried fruit.
★ White flour should be replaced by freshly ground wholemeal flours.
★ Fresh herbs and spices should be used regularly and often instead of salt.
★ Avoid chemically preserved foods and those containing synthetic additives.
★ For drinks, choose teas, milk, vegetable and fruit juices and mineral water.
★ In preparing your ingredients, remember the following basic idea; keep your food *fresh, simple and perfect as possible.*

The Composition of Good Foods

Protein — the Vital Ingredient for Living

Protein is actually the supoorter of life. Body cells as well as the blood and numerous hormones need protein to regulate vital metabolic processes. For this reason protein is an exceptional substance, although it can be replaced by fat and carbohydrates as a supplier of energy. The body consists of about 20 per cent protein, which is constantly being used up and must therefore be constantly replaced. Since the body cannot store protein, it must be taken in the daily diet.

Used and decomposed protein is mainly discharged through the kidneys and in the urine. In this way, 30-40g of used up protein leaves the body daily. *At least* this amount must then be replaced in the body to restore the balance. Authoritative organizations (among them the World Health Organization) recommend an intake of 0.9-1g of protein per kilo of body weight. This means that a person weighing 70 kilos should have a daily intake of 65-70g. Infants, children and adolescents, as well as pregnant women, nursing mothers and old people need extra protein.

During periods of growth, a lot of protein is required and is quickly used up. In the case of elderly people, the recommended intake is higher, since the body undergoes more wear and tear, the rate of decomposition of protein is quicker and it must be replaced accordingly. In addition, protein gives old people extra strength and supports the body's own system of defence against illness. Also adults who take little exercise and people whose work is mainly mental rather than physical should all have plenty of protein. To maintain a balance, fat, and above all, carbohydrate intake can then be but down, for these two substances are partly responsible for the overweight of 40 per cent of the population. On a diet of 2000-2500 calories per day, the proportion of protein should be about 80-90g.

Protein is made up of approximately twenty smaller elements. Some of these can be made by the body itself — these are non-essential amino acids. The rest — essential amino acids — must be taken daily in sufficient quantities. Not all proteins have the same value — it depends entirely on the amino acid composition.

As a rule, animal proteins tend to resemble those of the body more closely and are therefore of considerable importance in the human diet.

However it is now known that the quality of animal protein can also be achieved by combining two types of vegetable protein. One particularly good combination is that of egg and potato proteins; this is even more nourishing than the protein of chicken, which was always considered to be the best protein form of all. Various types of protein are found in all protein-rich foods, e.g., milk, cheese, eggs, meat or wholemeal bread. All of these have a different composition; for instance, one type of protein may lack just those elements which are present in great quantities in another form. In this way, it becomes a matter of combining the necessary elements of protein for optimum effect.

Protein can only be built up properly in the body if all the vital elements flow from the intestine to the liver at the same time. For this reason it is important to combine protein-rich foods within one meal, and this can occur when bread, milk, Quark and potatoes or soya products and eggs are eaten in combination.

Fat — the Great Supplier of Calories

Over the years our diet has included more and more fat. In the past ninety years fat consumption has risen from 15 to between 40 and 45 per cent of the total calorie intake.

It is now widely known that too many and incorrect types of fat in the diet are responsible for such illnesses as obesity and heart disease.

Like protein, fat consists of single elements, and as other foods these must be broken down by the digestive system. They are made up of a combination of glycerine and three fatty acids, these incidentally can differ enormously. The fatty acids may be divided into saturated, unsaturated and polyunsaturated types. Vegetable fats are mainly found in seeds and in fruit pulps. Animal fats are generally produced in the form of lard, and are distributed in and around the organs of the animal; they are also found in milk and egg yolk.

The generally high consumption of fats stems largely from the intake of foodstuffs with hidden fats. It is a good idea to use recognized fatty foods such as oil, butter and margarines sparingly. 'Dangerous' fats are those which one doesn't always recognize as such, for example, fatty meats, cheese, chocolate, sweets, cream products, cakes, etc.

In a daily allowance of 2000-2500 calories the recommended fat intake is 40g per day, in contrast with the actual consumption of between 70 and 80g per day. For the individual this means; be more choosy about one's food intake!

However, it is not just the question of the *amount* of energy-giving fats one eats, but also of their quality and the number of essential nutrients they contain. Since the body cannot synthesize these nutrients itself, they must be supplied daily through the diet. These essential elements include polyunsaturated linoleic acid, vitamins A, D and E and other vital components. Cholesterol and lecithin are also included in this category. The group of polyunsaturated fatty acids (the foremost of which is linoleic acid) together with vitamin E are of great importance to the body; they activate the combustion of fats, promote the combustion process which takes place within the cells and influence the body's handling of cholesterol. The choice of edible fats and oils is not only governed by their content of polyunsaturated acids but also by their means of processing. In the production of oil, a distinction is drawn between 'solvent extraction', 'hot-pressed processing' and 'cold-pressed processing'. In solvent extraction and hot-pressed processing the output is considerably higher, but oils extracted in this way have to undergo a refining process. This means that undesirable solvents are discarded along with other elements produced by heat and pressure; unfortunately, however — and this is the deciding factor — many of the valuable fat components such as fat-soluble vitamins, lecithin, natural colourings and smells are also refined out in the process.

A cold-pressed oil does not need to be processed in this way and therefore retains all its original elements. Cold-pressed oils also require a careful selection of raw ingredients and consequently these oils usually contain more polyunsaturates. A wide range of these oils is available in health food stores.

A few points could be made on the choice of margarines. 'Natural' margarines are preferable since they are free from chemically hardened fats, cholesterol and cooking salt; they also contain 15 per cent cold-pressed oil.

The following table shows percentage amounts of the various compositions of edible fats:

	Saturated Fatty Acids	Unsaturated Fatty Acids	Polyunsaturated Fatty Acids
Sunflower Oil	7	27	60
Linseed Oil	10	18	70
Thistle Oil	10	15	75
Corn Oil	17	32	50-60
Vegetable Margarine	33	22	45
Ordinary Table Margarine	Very high percentage	—	5-10
Coconut Fat	18	80	2
Butter	37	30	2- 5
Lard	41	45	8

Carbohydrate — the Bulk of Our Diet

In past years the proportion of carbohydrate in our diet has fallen from 76 to about 50 per cent. At the same time as fewer potatoes and cereals were consumed, there was a steady increase in the amount of sugar eaten. This is detrimental to health since sugar is an isolated, refined and concentrated carbohydrate which contains nothing which the body needs. Doctors and experts on nutrition give forceful warnings about sugar since it can contribute to the development of diet-related disorders.

In a proper diet, 50-55 per cent of the total calorie intake should consist of carbohydrate. On average, this is equivalent to about ¾ lb (350g) per day — supplied in the form of fruit (fresh and dried), vegetables including potatoes, wholegrain products and natural sweetening agents, though not in the form of refined sugar and sweeteners.

What is Meant by Carbohydrates?

The term 'carbohydrates' covers a range of organic compositions. Carbohydrates can be produced by plants through the effect of sunlight, and so they may be regarded as a good source of carbohydrate.

Monosaccharides: Dextrose (grape-sugar) and fructose are found in fruits and honey. They are used in a pure and concentrated form as sweeteners in cooking and drinks. Levulose is a component of lactose and cannot be bought in an isolated form. Monosaccharides can be absorbed directly into the blood from the intestines without additional digestion; the blood sugar level is thereby rapidly increased.

Disaccharides: Raw cane and beet-sugar in a pure and concentrated form is the type most widely used for cooking. It consists of dextrose and fructose.

Lactose is the carbohydrate of milk; this is often forgotten and people think that milk is just a source of protein.

Maltose is found in beer and the germ of barley. Malt extract may also be taken in a concentrated form.

Polysaccharides: Potatoes, bread, flour, rice and vegetables are the foods which contain polysaccharides in the form of starch, cellulose or pectin. In the liver polysaccharides are found in the form of glycogen.

If carbohydrate is eaten in this form, the polysaccharides must be broken down into their individual elements by the digestive system. Carbohydrates are the most important sources of energy; in fact they provide fewer calories than fat (1g of fat = 9.3 calories whereas 1g carbohydrate = 4.1 calories), yet they are of more significance. If one eats more carbohydrates than the body needs, they are converted into deposits of fat.

Sugar Types and their Peculiarities

Dextrose occurs naturally in fruits, fruit products and honey. Once eaten it is immediately incorporated into the blood and causes a rapid rise in the level of blood sugar. In cases of muscular activity dextrose is particularly useful and is also burned up quickly.

Sportsmen who often take dextrose in its isolated form before competitions should be aware that it is more valuable in natural combinations (for example, in the form of dried fruits, nut slices and natural sweeteners such as honey and fruit concentrates among many others).

This sugar plays an even greater part in the nutrition of infants and school children. Fresh and dried fruits, natural juices and sweeteners should always be present in the diet. As well as dextrose, these foods contain a plentiful supply of vital nutrients, whereas pure dextrose contains none.

At the same time it is worth considering that a rapid rise in the blood sugar level can also be detrimental. This happens when little energy is required in cases of minimal physical activity. A quick and plentiful supply of insulin must be available to flush the dextrose out of the blood into the cells and to convert it into fat. In addition, it should be said that a heavy production of insulin can easily lead to a low blood sugar level and this in turn creates a feeling of hunger.

Sucrose as a disaccharide consists of dextrose and fructose. Its sweetness is greater than that of dextrose but it is not as sweet as fructose.

This sugar is, without doubt, the cause of one of the greatest nutritional problems (the average consumption of sugar is estimated at about 4 oz/100g per day). It is relatively cheap, is contained in a hidden form in many food products and also tastes good.

Like dextrose and fructose this sugar contains no essential nutrients; it thus supplies the body with empty calories which take the place of other valuable foods. This leads to a lack of vitamins and minerals and plays a part in the development of certain illnesses. For this reason it is always a good idea to cut down drastically on the intake of such sugar. It is also worth trying to accustom the palate to less sweet food and gradually to introduce into the diet natural sweeteners such as honey, apple and pear concentrates, molasses and maple syrup.

Lactose is hardly sweet at all and is therefore not used as a sweetener. It is useful in that it is converted into lactic acid in the intestine, thereby promoting the growth of valuable intestinal bacteria. Moreover, an increase in the level of lactic acid within the intestine helps to eliminate harmful bacteria. Lactose also plays a great part in the nutrition of babies and young children when it is used to overcome constipation from which they often suffer.

High-fibre Foods

Originally it was thought that these foods played no significant part in the diet. This is now known to be incorrect and scientists have increasingly recognized the essential function of this substance.

Dietary fibre is indigestible, which means that it passes straight through the intestine without being taken up by the blood. It releases no nutrients and for this reason cannot cause overweight. Within the intestine, however, it performs an exceptionally important role. It absorbs water and is capable of swelling up to five times its original size, thereby increasing the contents of the intestine and irritating its muscular walls. Peristalsis is stimulated and digestion is accelerated.

In addition, mucous substances which are given off by the dietary fibre as it passes through the intestine have a favourable effect. They cover the sensitive walls of the intestine with a protective coating, enabling the contents of the intestine to slip through. It is interesting to note that an English nutritionist Prof Denis Burkitt has observed how the time it takes for intestinal contents to pass through is shortened when high-fibre foods are present. Europeans whose diets consist largely of low-fibre white flour products show a considerably longer time passing foods from the intestine in comparison with Africans whose diets are high in fibre. The longer the walls of the intestine are in contact with a decomposing stool, the greater the risk of inflammation developing.

The Essential Vitamins, Minerals and Trace Elements

Our nutrition is based on the substances protein, fat and carbohydrate. But man cannot survive on these nutrients alone; they must be complemented by vitamins, minerals and trace elements. It is true that these do not supply energy, but they play a decisive part in the transformation of foods to energy.

Vitamins, minerals and trace elements are *essential nutrients,* i.e., the body cannot produce them itself and, since they are vital for survival, a certain daily intake of them must be ensured to maintain health.

Vitamins

These are substances for which the body requires only very small amounts, sometimes only fractions of a milligram. They maintain certain structures and functions of the body and are therefore indispensable.

Certain vitamins can be formed within the intestine, but only with the help of bacteria. Whether this form of vitamin synthesis makes a significant contribution to the needs of the body is uncertain.

Each vitamin has special functions; however, since all vitamins are involved in general metabolism, it is impossible to draw clear distinctions — each vitamin is irreplaceable.

The vitamins are divided into two groups: *Fat-soluble vitamins*: Vitamins A, D, E and K; and *Water-soluble vitamins*: Vitamins B_1, B_2, Niacin, B_6, pantothenic acid, inositol, choline, folic acid, B_{12} and vitamin C.

Where they occur:

Vitamin A — Liver, fish oils, milk, eggs, some margarines.
Carotene (provitamin A) — Fruit, vegetables.
Vitamin D — Fish oils, liver, egg yolk, milk and milk products.
Vitamin E — Vegetable oils (wheatgerm oil), leafy vegetables, liver, eggs, milk and milk products.
Vitamin K — Liver, vegetables.
Vitamin B_1 — Whole grains, wheatgerm, liver, yeast, pork, vegetables, milk, potatoes, soya beans and nuts.
Vitamin B_2 — Yeast and yeast products, milk and milk products, wheatgerm, whole grains, meat, vegetables and potatoes.

Vitamin B$_6$ — Whole grains, soya flour, yeast, liver, potatoes and vegetables.
Niacin — Whole grains, liver and yeast.
Folic acid — Whole grains, yeast, liver and vegetables.
Pantothenic acid — Whole grains, liver, vegetables and eggs.
Vitamin B$_{12}$ — Milk and milk products, liver.
Vitamin C — Fruit (e.g., sea buckthorn*, acerola cherries, black currants, rosehips). Vegetables (e.g., red peppers, *Sauerkraut* and potatoes).

An inadequate intake of vitamins may arise through a lack of variety in the diet; a high intake of foods such as white bread, white flour, tinned goods, sugar etc.; destruction of vitamins through incorrect storage before foods are prepared; possibly through a weakness in today's ability to absorb vitamins.

Vitamins Are Very Sensitive!

Vitamins are highly sensitive to light, oxygen, acids, heat and water — all factors to which foodstuffs are generally exposed before consumption. In normal food preparation, for example, 20 per cent of the vitamin B, and 50 per cent of the vitamin C is lost. It is therefore not just the choice of foods but also their preparation which is of vital importance (see page 17).

Minerals and Trace Elements

These substances help to develop organic structures; they deal with the distribution of fluids and are responsible for the body's osmotic balance. Minerals or trace elements are also constituents of enzymes which control the rate of metabolism. The human body is made up of between four and five per cent of minerals and trace elements.

A distinction is drawn between the sizes of the constituents:

Mass elements: Sodium, potassium, magnesium, calcium, phosphorous, chloride.
Trace elements: Chromium, iron, flouride, iodine, cobalt, copper, manganese, silicon, zinc.

Where they occur:

Sodium — Meat, sea salt.
Potassium — Fruit (fresh and dried), vegetables, potatoes, brown rice.
Magnesium — Green vegetables, fruit, potatoes, wheatgerm.
Calcium — Milk and milk products, fruit, vegetables.
Phosphorus — Milk and milk products, potatoes, whole grains, meat.
Chloride — Meat extracts, sea salt.
Iron — Meat, egg yolks, whole grains, fruit, vegetables, potatoes.
Flouride — Black tea, seafoods.
Iodine — Seafoods, eggs; the iodine content of vegetables etc. depends on iodine content of the soil in which the food was grown.

Most minerals and trace elements are supplied in adequate quantities. However, there is often an inadequate intake of iron and calcium.

On the other hand, most people include too much sodium and chloride in the form of salt in their diets. A high intake of salt can lead to water retention which places a great strain on the circulatory system. For this reason it is a good idea to use less salt and more herbs in cooking.

In contrast, potassium encourages the distribution of fluids in the body; this is why potassium-

*Available as a concentrate from *Weleda*.

1.   Elderberry Soup (page 38) and Quark-filled Pancake (page 131)

rich foods are recommended in cases of water retention (oedema).

An adequate intake of vitamins and minerals is ensured when as many fresh wholefoods as possible are included in the diet; these include milk and milk products, whole grains and wholegrain products, fruit and vegetables and cold-pressed vegetable oils. Complementary to these foods are yeast products, wheatgerm, bran and natural fruit concentrates.

Buying and Storing Foods

The value of food is measured in terms of how much it can contribute to total nutrition and the maintenance of health. The foods which are the most valuable are those with a high content of essential nutrients (essential amino acids, fatty acids, vitamins, minerals) and as few additives as possible. The most important factors are: careful selection of wholefoods; ecologically cultivated foods; unadulteration of foods through correct storage and careful processing where necessary.

Nevertheless, a food's value depends not only on the state in which it is bought but also on the state in which it is eaten. It is often forgotten that it is those very health-giving constituents of certain foods which can be particularly sensitive to light, oxygen, heat and water. Careless preparation of foods in the kitchen can lead to a high loss of nutrients and the food's value is then greatly reduced.

Fresh Fruit and Vegetables

Before being bought, foods should be looked at for their freshness. Fruit, vegetables and herbs have only a short shelf life; for example there is a 20 per cent reduction in the vitamin C content of spinach after only 24 hours. Good storage places include the vegetable compartment of a refrigerator or a dark, cool, well-aired room. Leafy vegetables may also be kept in tin foil or air-tight containers. Herbs stay fresh longer if kept in the fridge or again in an air-tight container.

Water can cause vital water-soluble nutrients to dissolve out of certain foods, as in the case of vitamins B_1 and C, various minerals, trace elements and protein. For this reason, vegetables should always be washed in a bowl or sink of cold water rather than under the tap. Do not leave fruit and vegetables to stand in water and only chop them into pieces *after* they have been washed. In chopping vegetables and fruit a greater surface area is produced and water, air and heat can thereby do more damage. When handling lettuce and other salad vegetables, for instance, always wash the leaves first and then chop or tear them into pieces.

Above all, the vitamins A and C can be destroyed by exposure to oxygen; vitamin A is also very sensitive to light. This is why raw fruit and vegetables should only be prepared shortly before they are served, unless in exceptional cases they can be prepared and kept in the fridge in air-tight containers or aluminium foil.

Excessive cooking temperatures or prolonged heating can also cause considerable loss of nutrients. Therefore foods should be stewed, steamed, grilled or baked in foil rather than boiled. A pressure cooker is recommended for this type of cooking. There are also many advantages to a microwave oven although there is still some controversy over its possible hazards. The length of time a meal is cooked for and kept warm has a great effect on its vitamin content. If the early preparation of some meals is unavoidable it is best to let the food cool down as soon as it is prepared and then warm it up when needed, rather than leave it cooking.

Basic Guidelines for Preparing Fruit and Vegetables

★ Preparation should be done as near to serving as possible. Scrub away as little as possible

2. Mueslis

from the fruit or vegetable when cleaning or peeling.
*   Wash very briefly; do not leave to soak in water.
*   *After* washing, chop into large rather than small pieces.
*   Choose the right temperature for cooking and cook for as short a time as possible.
*   Avoid keeping food warm for long periods.
*   Keep food in a cool place if it is to be heated up again later.

The most suitable fruit and vegetables for long storage are apples and pears, carrots, celeriac, beetroot and potatoes. Of course some important nutrients are also lost in storing fruit and vegetables, but a certain amount of natural protection is provided by the peel; in the past these were the only winter fruit available. For good storage the room should be cool but not cold, airy and dry.

Freezing Fruit and Vegetables

Of all the methods of preserving food, deep freezing has the most advantages. It has become established in recent years and frozen foods are said to have a high nutritional value. Whenever good fresh foods are unavailable deep frozen foods are the next best thing. Frozen goods must be prepared for the freezer within a few hours of being picked, in the case of fruit and vegetables. If necessary, the foods should be blanched (dipped in boiling water for 1 to 3 minutes and then cooled briefly under cold water). They should also be packed and frozen correctly at temperatures of between 18 and 40 degrees.

Milk and Milk Products

Milk and milk products are almost indispensable ingredients in wholefood cooking. Milk is available in various forms:

Pasteurized — the milk is heated for 40 seconds at 71°C/158°F to sterilize it. It may be kept refrigerated for a few days.
U.H.T. — the milk is heated for 2-3 seconds at 135-150°C/275-300°F. Through this brief heat treatment and immediate cooling the milk is preserved and will keep for up to 6 weeks.
Flavoured Milk Drinks — these are available in cocoa and fruit flavours and are usually heavily sweetened.

Soured Milk Products

Soured Milk — this is made with various types of milk; bacteria cultures are used to begin the souring process. Soured milks are either runny or set.
Yogurt — unlike other soured milk products this is prepared with certain fermenting substances. It is available in several forms — runny or set and with various fat contents.
Flavoured yogurts — contain fruit but also sweeteners, flavouring, colouring and other additives.
Buttermilk — a by-product in butter production.
Whey — a by-product in cheese making. It contains valuable protein, and is rich in minerals and vitamins. Whey has a neutral taste and combines well with fruit.
Quark — made from milk using lactic acid bacteria. It contains plenty of protein as well as considerable amounts of calcium phosphorus and vitamin A. It is a versatile ingredient to use in cooking and is economical too.
Cheese — it is difficult to imagine vegetarian cooking without this ingredient. It is a good supplier of protein, although this depends somewhat on its fat content; the fattier the cheese, the less protein it contains.

Cream — obtained by skimming the top of the milk. There is a difference in the fat content of double cream (30 per cent) and soured cream (10 per cent). Used in small quantities (on account of its high calorific value), these products may be used to enhance the flavours of wholefood cooking.

Storing Milk and Milk Products

Since milk does not stay fresh long it should be stored carefully: Milk reacts when exposed to air, warmth or light, therefore remember the following points:

★ Do not leave to stand uncovered for long periods.
★ Keep away from heat.
★ Do not stand milk in the light (daylight or artificial).
★ Milk and milk products *must* be stored in a cool place.
★ Long-life milk and sterilized milk go off once the packet or bottle is opened (without tasting sour). Always use them up quickly once opened.

Cereals and Cereal Products

Providing grain is not kibbled, ground or rolled, it may be kept for years. The shelf life of cereal products, however, is more limited. Wheatgerm, for example, is so sensitive to oxygen that were it not stabilized it would be ruined after just a few hours' exposure. Freshly ground grain should not be stored for more than a few days, whereas flaked cereals and ready-made mueslis may be kept for several months.

Wholemeal bread goes mouldy quite quickly, especially in humid weather conditions. For this reason, loaves should be kept somewhere airy, cool and dry. Bread which has already turned slightly mouldy should never be eaten or fed to animals. Freezing is an ideal way to store bread.

Cooking Fats

The length of time certain cooking oils and fats may be kept for varies considerably since they are sensitive to warmth, light, oxygen and smell. They should therefore be stored covered in a cool, dark place. Fats which contain water, such as vegetable margarines and butter, may be kept for short periods, preferably refrigerated. Blocks of fat such as coconut and palm nut may be kept wrapped in a cool place for months.

Cooking oils, if stored unopened in favourable conditions, will keep for 6 to 12 months, with the exception of linseed oil which will keep for 12 weeks if unopened. For this reason, linseed and other speciality oils are available in small quantities at health food stores. Once opened oils should generally be used within 4 to 6 weeks; linseed oil within 10 to 12 days.

Useful Ingredients for Wholefood Cooking

Agar-agar — Produced from seaweeds and contains a high proportion of minerals. Used instead of gelatine in vegetarian dishes and is ideal for jam making.
Apple concentrate — Combines well with sweet and sour dishes and in small quantities is good in salad dressings.
Bran — A by-product of flour production, contains a high proportion of indigestible fibre which swells in the intestine and promotes peristalsis to cut down the time it takes for food to pass through the body.
Dried fruit — Contains in a concentrated form the valuable substances of fruit. They should

Bran Muesli

Serves 1 P 10g, F 6g, C 47g, Cals 370

Imperial (Metric)

6 fl oz (170ml) soured milk
2-3 tablespoonsful wheat bran
1 teaspoonful wheatgerm
2 oz (50g) dried fruit, soaked
A little lemon juice

1. Place the milk in a bowl and stir briefly, then add the bran and wheatgerm.
2. Chop up the dried fruit and add it to the mixture with lemon juice to taste.

Quark and Fruit Muesli

Serves 1 P 23g, F 9g, C 20g, Cals 266

Imperial (Metric)

4 oz (100g) Quark
3-4 tablespoonsful milk
1 teaspoonful bran
¾ oz (20g) nuts, ground
A little honey
4 oz (100g) pineapple or other fruit

1. Mix the Quark with the milk until smooth.
2. Add the bran, nuts and honey to taste.
3. Stir in the cubed pineapple or other fruit.

Millet Flake Muesli

Serves 1   P 13g, F 13g, C 45g, Cals 370

Imperial (Metric)

6 fl oz (170ml) natural yogurt or soured milk
½ oz (15g) hazelnuts, ground
4 oz (100g) seasonal fruit
1 teaspoonful honey
A little lemon juice
4-5 tablespoonsful millet flakes

1. Place the yogurt or milk in a bowl and stir in the nuts and chopped or grated fruit.
2. Add honey and lemon juice to taste.
3. Finally stir in the millet just before serving to prevent it becoming soggy.

Porridge with Prunes

Serves 1   P 9g, F 8g, C 57g, Cals 338

Imperial (Metric)

½ pint (285ml) water
1½ oz (40g) jumbo oat flakes
2 oz (50g) prunes — approx. 5
Pinch of sea salt
A little single cream

1. Boil the water and add the oats. Leave to soak for approx. 20 minutes.
2. Add the soaked prunes and salt and sugar to taste.
3. Serve with cream if liked.

Buckwheat Porridge

Serves 4   P 1g, F 0.5g, C 40g, Cals 675

Imperial (Metric)

2 pints (1 litre) milk (or half milk half water)
5-6 oz (150-200g) buckwheat groats
Pinch sea salt
2 tablespoonsful honey

1. Bring the milk to the boil, add the buckwheat, bring back to boil and then leave to soak for 30-40 minutes.
2. Add salt and honey to taste. Serve with fruit if liked.

Note: This dish may be flavoured with herbs instead of honey.

Millet Porridge with Apricots

Serves 1   P 7g, F 4g, C 56g, Cals 286

Imperial (Metric)

1½-2 oz (40-50g) millet
¼ pint (150ml) water
2 tablespoonsful cream
Pinch of sea salt
1 teaspoonful honey
2 oz (50g) dried apricots, soaked

1. Stir the washed millet into the cold water and bring to the boil. Simmer for 10 minutes.
2. Add the cream and salt and honey to taste, then mix in the fruit.

Cottage Cheese with Apple

Serves 1   P 21g, F 7g, C 15g, Cals 222

Imperial (Metric)

6 oz (150g) cottage cheese
A little milk
4 oz (100g) grated apple
1-2 wholemeal crispbreads

1. Mix the cheese with a little milk and stir in the apple.
2. Spread the mixture on the crispbreads.

Cheesy Quark Spread

Serves 1   P 28g, F 8g, C 23g, Cals 297

Imperial (Metric)

4 oz (100g) Quark
Approx. 6 tablespoonsful milk
1 oz (25g) Roquefort or Gorgonzola cheese
Pinch sea salt
2 wholemeal crispbreads

1. Mix the Quark with the milk until smooth, then add the crumbled cheese.
2. Add the salt to taste and spread the mixture on the crispbreads.

2.
SOUPS, STARTERS AND SNACKS

A carefully chosen and well prepared soup may be used not only to begin a meal but to complete or balance a menu according to its ingredients. A vegetable soup with fresh herbs, for example, may be served before a casserole which provides few vitamins; in summer a high-protein Quark dish may be complemented by a refreshing cold fruit soup; or try serving a filling wholegrain soup before a light salad meal. Soups are also ideal as snacks or suppers on cold winter evenings.

Italian Vegetable Soup

Serves 4   P 1g, F 10g, C 6g, Cals 120

Imperial (Metric)

Approx. 14 oz (400g) vegetables (carrots, kohlrabi, celery, peas, cauliflower, leeks)
4 tablespoonsful vegetable oil
2 pints (1 litre) vegetable stock
Sea salt and freshly ground black pepper
Pinch each of mixed herbs and basil
1 bunch of parsley, chopped

1. Prepare the vegetables by washing, trimming and dicing them.
2. Lightly sauté them in hot oil, then pour on the stock.
3. Season with salt and pepper and add the herbs before serving.

Onion Soup

Serves 4   P 9g, F 11g, C 22g, Cals 227

Imperial (Metric)

14 oz (400g) onions
4 tablespoonsful vegetable oil
2-3 pints (1-1½ litres) vegetable stock
Freshly ground black pepper
1 bay leaf
Pinch of ground juniper
3-4 tablespoonsful white wine
4 thin slices wholemeal bread
4 oz (100g) grated Emmental cheese

1. Finely slice the onions and sauté them in the oil.
2. Gradually add the stock and slowly bring to the boil.
3. Add the seasoning and herbs, then pour in the wine.
4. Pour the soup into ovenproof bowls, top with the toasted bread and cheese and bake for approximately 10 minutes at 425°F/220°C (Gas Mark 7).

Spring Soup

Serves 4   P 7g, F 10g, C 17.5g, Cals 173

Imperial (Metric)

1 onion, finely diced
4 oz (100g) potato, grated
9 oz (250g) fresh spinach
1 oz (25g) vegetable margarine
1½ pints (¾ litre) vegetable stock
Sea salt and freshly ground black pepper
A little lemon juice
½ clove garlic, crushed
1 tablespoonful wholemeal flour
2 cartons natural yogurt
3-4 tablespoonsful fresh herbs, chopped

1. Sauté the onion, potato and spinach in the oil, then add the stock and simmer.
2. Season to taste with salt, pepper, lemon juice and garlic.
3. Bring to the boil then add a spoonful or two of the soup to the flour to make a paste. Stir in the flour mixture and simmer again.
4. Add the natural yogurt (except for 4 tablespoonsful) and stir well.
5. Place a spoonful of yogurt in each of the soup bowls before serving.

Note: This makes an ideal supper dish on a warm summer evening.

3.   Salad and Soup with Herbs

Quick Vegetable Soup

Serves 4   P 1g, F 2g, C 6g, Cals 45

Imperial (Metric)

2 pints (1 litre) vegetable stock
10 oz (300g) frozen mixed vegetables
Parsley, chopped

1. Bring the stock to the boil and add the frozen vegetables.
2. Bring to the boil and simmer for 10-12 minutes.
3. Pour the soup into bowls and sprinkle with parsley.

Buckwheat Soup

Serves 4   P 4g, F 10g, C 22g, Cals 200

Imperial (Metric)

4 oz (100g) buckwheat
2 pints (1 litre) vegetable stock
3 tablespoonsful vegetable oil
6 oz (150g) onions, chopped
Nutmeg
Sea salt and freshly ground black pepper
Celery salt and garlic powders
Oregano
1 oz (25g) grated cheese
Chives to garnish

1. Coarsely grind the buckwheat and soak it for approximately 1 hour in the stock.
2. Heat the oil and sauté the onions, then pour on the stock and simmer for 25 minutes.
3. Season with nutmeg, salt, pepper, celery salt, garlic powder and oregano and top with the cheese and chives before serving.

4. Savoury Toasts (pages 43-4)

Wheat and Leek Soup

Serves 4   P 2g, F 4g, C 14g, Cals 100

Imperial (Metric)

1 oz (25g) vegetable margarine
1 medium onion, diced
2½ oz (65g) coarsely ground wheat
2 pints (1 litre) water
1 leek, sliced
1 teaspoonful yeast extract
Sea salt and freshly ground black pepper
1 bunch of parsley, chopped

1. Heat the fat and sauté the onions and wheat, then pour on the water.
2. Add the leeks and simmer for 20-25 mintues.
3. Season with the remaining ingredients and top with plenty of parsley before serving.

Simple Barley Soup

Serves 4   P 2g, F 6g, C 20g, Cals 145

Imperial (Metric)

3 tablespoonsful vegetable margarine
1 onion, diced
1 small leek, finely chopped
3-4 oz (75-100g) pot barley
2 pints (1 litre) water
1 carrot, diced
Sea salt and freshly ground black pepper
Nutmeg
1 vegetable stock cube

1. Heat the margarine and sauté the onion and leek, then add the barley, water and carrot.
2. Simmer for 20-30 minutes and season to taste.

Millet Soup

Serves 4   P 3g, F 8g, C 20g, Cals 175

Imperial (Metric)

3 tablespoonsful vegetable oil
4 oz (100g) carrots, finely diced
1 parsley root, diced
2 pints (1 litre) water
1 teaspoonful yeast extract
4 oz (100g) millet
Sea salt and freshly ground black pepper

1. Heat the vegetable oil and sauté the carrots and parsley root.
2. Pour on the water, season with yeast extract and add the washed millet.
3. Simmer for 20-30 minutes and add a little salt and pepper to taste.

Potato Soup

Serves 4   *Illustrated opposite page 96*   P 5g, F 7g, C 22g, Cals 180

Imperial (Metric)

1 lb (½ kilo) potatoes
2 pints (1 litre) vegetable stock
1 medium onion, diced
4 oz (100g) leeks, finely chopped
1 tablespoonful vegetable margarine
Sea salt and freshly ground black pepper
Marjoram
1 egg yolk
3 tablespoonsful milk
1 tablespoonful flaked almonds

1. Peel and dice the potatoes, cook them in the stock until soft, then mash them or
    blend in a liquidizer.
2. Sauté the onion and leeks in the margarine, add them to the soup and season well.
3. Mix together the egg yolk and milk and use it to thicken the soup.
4. Sprinkle with the almonds before serving.

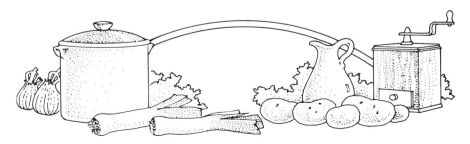

Imperial (Metric)

1 glass pure fruit juice with
1 tablespoonful wheatgerm added
2 wholemeal crispbreads

Other Suggestions:
Raw carrots, slices of cucumber, bean sprouts, radishes, tomatoes, apples, peaches, pears,
  strawberries, bananas, or oranges all make ideal snacks. Also try low-fat cheese and
  savoury Quark mixtures with wholemeal bread or crispbreads and various vegetable
  juices. Milk drinks (pages 144-149) are particularly suitable for summer.

3.
MAIN DISHES

Hearty Casseroles

Casserole dishes are ideal meals to prepare in advance for warming up later. They are easy to serve and provide great scope for combining various ingredients. Casseroles make filling main meals or may be used to enrich soups. Always try to add a wide range of vegetables and whole grains to casseroles and only add chopped herbs at the end of cooking time. The pans or dishes used should have tight-fitting lids to reduce cooking time and preserve the vitamin content.

Vegetable Casserole

Serves 4   P 22g, F 31g, C 23g, Cals 494

Imperial (Metric)

½ lb (¼ kilo) potatoes
1 lb (½ kilo) carrots
½ celeriac
1 leek
2 medium onions
½ Savoy cabbage
3 tablespoonsful vegetable oil
2 pints (1 litre) vegetable stock
Sea salt and freshly ground black pepper
2 tablespoonsful yeast flakes
1 bunch of parsley

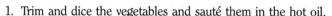

1. Trim and dice the vegetables and sauté them in the hot oil.
2. Pour on the stock and simmer in a covered pan for 30 minutes.
3. Add the salt, pepper and yeast flakes and top with the freshly chopped parsley.

French Bean Casserole

Serves 4   P 19g, F 8g, C 52g, Cals 390

Imperial (Metric)

½ lb (¼ kilo) haricot beans, soaked
1 leek, sliced
4 oz (100g) onions, diced
Sea salt and freshly ground black pepper
1-2 bay leaves
2-3 pints (1-1½ litres) vegetable stock
½ lb (¼ kilo) onions
2 tablespoonsful vegetable oil
1 lb (½ kilo) tomatoes, skinned
2 cloves garlic, crushed
Thyme
¼ pint (150ml) dry white wine
2 oz (50g) grated cheese

1. Simmer the beans, leek and diced onions with the bay leaves in the well seasoned vegetable stock for 60-70 minutes.
2. Finely chop the remaining onions and sauté them in the oil.
3. Quarter the tomatoes and add them to the onions with the garlic, thyme and wine.
4. Leave to stand for a while then combine the two mixtures and season to taste again.
5. Bake in a greased casserole, topped with cheese if liked.

Beetroot Casserole

Serves 4   P 5g, F 10g, C 25g, Cals 200

Imperial (Metric)

1½ lb (¾ kilo) beetroot
½ lb (¼ kilo) carrots
½ lb (¼ kilo) onions
4 tablespoonsful vegetable oil
Approx. 2 pints (1 litre) water
A little yeast extract
1-2 bay leaves
Sea salt and freshly ground black pepper
1 clove garlic
A little lemon juice

1. Peel the vegetables and slice or dice them.
2. Sauté them in the hot oil and pour on the yeast stock.
3. Season to taste with the remaining ingredients and simmer until the vegetables are soft.

Barley Casserole

Serves 4   P 4g, F 8g, C 35g, Cals 240

Imperial (Metric)

Approx. 1 lb (½ kilo) carrots
1 medium onion
4 tablespoonsful vegetable oil
Approx. 5 oz (125g) pot barley, soaked for 3-4 hours
Approx. 2-3 pints (1-1½ litres) water
teaspoonful yeast extract
Sea salt and freshly ground black pepper
Celery leaves

1. Peel and dice the carrots and onion and sauté them in the hot vegetable oil.
2. Add the barley and the water and season with the remaining ingredients, except for the celery leaves.
3. Bring to the boil, then simmer for 40-50 minutes.
4. Garnish with the chopped leaves just before serving.

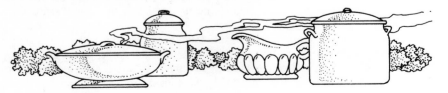

5.   A natural foods buffet

Chick Pea Casserole

Serves 4   P 18g, F 10g, C 70g, Cals 460

Imperial (Metric)

½ lb (¼ kilo) chick peas, soaked overnight
3 pints (1½ litres) water with a little yeast extract
4 tablespoonsful vegetable oil
2 medium onions, diced
3-4 cloves garlic
2 large carrots, diced
1 large tin tomatoes
4 medium potatoes, diced
Pinch each of basil, rosemary and thyme
Cayenne pepper
Sea salt and freshly ground black pepper
2 tablespoonsful chopped parsley

1. Bring the chick peas to the boil using the water, then simmer for about 1 hour.
2. Meanwhile heat the oil and sauté the onions, garlic and carrots.
3. Add the tomatoes (with the juice) and the potatoes.
4. Simmer the vegetable mixture for 20 minutes, then add it to the chick peas.
5. Cook thoroughly and season to taste, then garnish with the parsley.

Lentil Casserole

Serves 4   P 20g, F 4g, C 75g, Cals 420

Imperial (Metric)

Approx. ½ lb (¼ kilo) lentils
1 bunch of parsley
4 medium potatoes
2 medium onions
1-2 leeks
1-2 teaspoonsful cider vinegar or 3 tablespoonsful red wine
Sea salt and freshly ground black pepper
A little yeast extract
Thyme
Marjoram
1 carton soured cream
2 tablespoonsful chopped parsley

1. Soak the lentils overnight then bring them to the boil in the soaking water.
2. Meanwhile trim and dice the vegetables except for the leeks and add them to the lentils. Simmer for 50-60 minutes over a very low heat.
3. After about 30 minutes add the sliced leeks together with the vinegar or wine and seasoning.
4. Serve this dish in deep bowls with a dessertspoonful of cream and some parsley.

6. Soya Rissoles (page 52) and Wheat Salad with Green Pepper and Cucumber (page 113)

New Ideas for Soya

The soya bean belongs botanically to the legume family. It originated in Asia and is now mainly grown in the U.S.A. It is particularly useful due to its high protein content (38 per cent) and its versatility, which makes it an increasingly valuable crop throughout the world; also it is an important meat substitute in vegetarian cooking.

A distinction is made between green and yellow soya beans; the green beans are known as mung and are primarily used for sprouting, whereas the yellow beans are processed to make many different products. Soya flour is well known, as are soya chunks (for use in goulash, casserole and cabbage dishes), and soya sausages and pâtés. The latter are available tinned and need no preparation, whereas the meat substitutes require some soaking.

Soya products are high in protein, relatively low in fat and contain no cholesterol and thereby have genuine advantages in terms of healthy eating.

Stuffed Onions

Serves 4   P 22g, F 15g, C 22g, Cals 300

Imperial (Metric)

4 large onions
4 oz (100g) soya 'mince', soaked
1 egg
1-2 tablespoonsful real soya sauce
2-3 tablespoonsful wholemeal breadcrumbs
Sea salt and freshly ground black pepper
Paprika
Marjoram
1 bunch of parsley, chopped

1. Cook the peeled onions whole for about 10 minutes in salted water.
2. Remove the onions, allow them to drain and remove the centres.
3. Chop up the pieces of onion and mix it with the soya 'mince', egg, sauce, breadcrumbs, seasoning and herbs.
4. Spoon the mixture into the onions and bake them for 30-40 minutes in an ovenproof dish, (if necessary with a little liquid).

Note: Serve with brown rice and a tomato sauce.

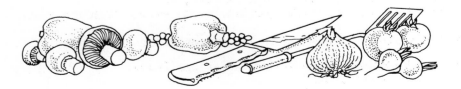

Soya and Vegetable Casserole

Serves 4   P 23g, F 15g, C 14g, Cals 290

Imperial (Metric)

4-6 oz (100-150g) soya 'mince'
1 teaspoonful yeast extract dissolved in ½ pint (¼ litre) liquid
1 tablespoonful vegetable margarine
1 medium onion, finely chopped
Sea salt and freshly ground black pepper
1 lb (½ kilo) mixed vegetables, fresh or frozen
1 medium onion or 2 shallots
1 bay leaf
A little onion powder
Pinch of nutmeg
2 eggs
3 tablespoonsful milk
2 tablespoonsful vegetable margarine or butter
1 oz (25g) sunflower seeds

1. Soak the 'mince' in the yeast extract stock for about 20 minutes. Strain it thoroughly and sauté in the margarine with the onion. Season to taste.
2. Prepare the vegetables, dicing them if necessary, and simmer them with the chopped onion or shallots in a small amount of liquid.
3. Add seasoning and mix the vegetables with the soya mixture. Place in a greased casserole dish.
4. Whisk the eggs and milk and pour over the casserole. Dot with butter and sprinkle on the seeds and bake at 400°F/200°C (Gas Mark 6) for approximately 30 minutes.

Note: Serve with creamed potatoes and green salad.

Millet Casserole

Serves 4 P 18g, F 14g, C 44g, Cals 376

Imperial (Metric)

2 tablespoonsful vegetable oil
1 small onion, chopped
7 oz (200g) millet
1 pint (½ litre) hot water with a little yeast extract dissolved in it
Sea salt and freshly ground black pepper
1 bay leaf
7 oz (200g) button mushrooms
7 oz (200g) peas, frozen or par-boiled
1 clove garlic, crushed
1 tablespoonful soya flour
2 eggs
2 tablespoonsful skimmed milk powder
4 tablespoonsful water
Nutmeg
2 oz (50g) grated cheese

1. Heat the oil and briefly sauté the onion and the washed millet.
2. Add the hot liquid, seasoning and bay leaf and cook in a covered pan for approximately 15 minutes over a low heat.
3. Mix in the mushrooms, peas, garlic and flour.
4. Whisk together the eggs, milk powder, water and seasoning and pour the mixture over the millet.
5. Place the mixture in a greased casserole and sprinkle with cheese, then bake for about 15 minutes at 450°F/230°C (Gas Mark 8). Serve with assorted salads.

Kibbled Wheat Casserole

Serves 4 — P 14g, F 14g, C 26g, Cals 407

Imperial (Metric)

6 oz (150g) carrots
6 oz (150g) celery
1 leek
3 tablespoonsful vegetable oil
¼ pint (150ml) hot water
1 tablespoonful yeast extract
1 pint (½ litre) milk
4-5 oz (100-125g) kibbled wheat
Sea salt and freshly ground black pepper
3 eggs, separated
1-2 tablespoonsful soya flour
1-2 tablespoonsful yeast flakes
2 oz (50g) grated cheese

1. Wash and dice the vegetables and sauté them briefly in hot oil.
2. Mix the water and yeast extract and add it to the pan, then bring to the boil.
3. Add the milk and wheat, bring back to the boil and allow to soak for 15-20 minutes.
4. Mix the seasoning, egg yolk, flour and yeast flakes.
5. Whisk the egg whites and fold them gently into the mixture. Sprinkle with cheese.
6. Bake for approximately 30 minutes at 425°F/220°C (Gas Mark 7) and serve with grilled tomatoes.

Sweet Wholewheat Dumplings

Serves 6 — P 12g, F 10g, C 65g, Cals 410

Imperial (Metric)

1 lb (½ kilo) whole wheat, kibbled wheat or wholemeal flour
1½ oz (40g) fresh yeast or 1 packet dried yeast
2 tablespoonsful raw cane sugar
½ pint (¼ litre) lukewarm milk
Pinch of sea salt
Pinch of cinnamon
2 oz (50g) vegetable margarine
¼ pint (150ml) lukewarm milk
Few drops of vanilla essence

1. If necessary, finely grind the wheat and make a well in the centre.
2. Mix the yeast with the sugar and add a little of the lukewarm milk and add it to the flour. Set aside for 20 minutes.
3. Combine the remaining milk, honey, salt, cinnamon and margarine to form a smooth batter and set aside for approximately 30 minutes.
4. Knead the two mixtures together and then form 8-10 dumplings. Set them out in a greased casserole and leave them in a warm place for a further 20 minutes.
5. Combine the second quantity of milk and the vanilla essence and pour the mixture over the dumplings.
6. Bake in a covered casserole for approximately 40 minutes at 400°F/200°C (Gas Mark 6), until the dumplings are golden brown and the milk has been absorbed.

Note: Serve with all kinds of fruit purées.

Sesame Waffles

Makes 8   P 9g, F 18g, C 25g, Cals 325

Imperial (Metric)

6 oz (150g) wholemeal flour
4 oz (100g) kibbled wheat
4 oz (100g) sesame seeds
½ packet dried yeast
Sea salt to taste
4 oz (100g) butter, melted
½ pint (¼ litre) milk
2-3 eggs
3-4 tablespoonsful honey

1. Combine the flour, kibbled wheat, half of the sesame seeds, yeast, salt, butter, milk, eggs and honey to form a smooth batter.
2. Set the mixture aside for 20-30 minutes.
3. Heat the waffle iron, grease it and sprinkle on the remaining seeds.
4. Spoon the mixture into the waffle iron and close the lid. Cook for 5-7 minutes on a medium heat.

Note: Waffles taste best when fresh and may be served at childrens parties, for Sunday breakfast or at any time with a fruit purée.

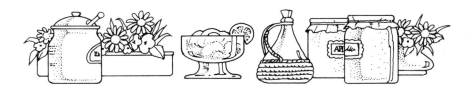

Rice

The rice grain has two outer layers; one is the hard, indigestible husk and the other is the silver skin which contains all the vitamins and minerals. Brown rice is always unpolished and retains its slightly brownish appearance even when boiled.

In contrast, white rice is polished and therefore lacking in important vitamins, minerals and fibre. White rice is less satisfying and therefore larger portions are required.

Rice-Basic Recipe

Serves 4   P 4g, F 6g, C 40g, Cals 241

Imperial (Metric)

7 oz (200g) brown rice
1 onion, chopped
2 tablespoonsful vegetable oil
1 pint (½ litre) vegetable stock
1 bay leaf
Sea salt and freshly ground black pepper

1. Wash the rice, allow it to drain and sauté it with the onion in the oil.
2. Bring the remaining ingredients to the boil and pour it over the rice. Cover the pan and allow the rice to simmer gently for 30-40 minutes.

Note: This recipe can be varied using all sorts of herbs and vegetables, for example, use peas to make Risi Bisi.

Rice Salad with Leeks

Serves 4   P 10g, F 13g, C 40g, Cals 270

Imperial (Metric)

4 oz (100g) long-grain brown rice, cooked
2 leeks, finely sliced
½ packet frozen peas, cooked
2 slices pineapple
4 oz (100g) Gouda cheese, diced

Dressing:
3 tablespoonsful sunflower oil
2 tablespoonsful fruit vinegar
Raw cane sugar
Sea salt and freshly ground black pepper
1 clove garlic, crushed
1 medium onion, chopped
1 tablespoonful chopped parsley

1. Mix together the rice and leeks with the peas, pineapple and cheese.
2. Combine the dressing ingredients to taste and mix it in with the salad.
3. Allow the flavours to mingle for a while before serving.

Polenta

Serves 4 · P 8g, F 1g, C 60g, Cals 281

Imperial (Metric)

1½-2 pints (¾-1 litre) water
1 teaspoonful sea salt
Pinch of raw cane sugar
½ lb (¼ kilo) maize flour (cornmeal)

1. Bring the salted water to the boil and sprinkle in the maize flour.
2. Stir well and simmer for approximately 20 minutes, being careful that the mixture doesn't burn.

Note: This dish may be served as a main meal when mixed with cheese, butter or freshly chopped herbs. It is also popular when added to stewed fruit or dried fruit which has been soaked.

Maize Waffles with Almonds

Makes 8 · P 8g, F 15g, C 30g, Cals 300

Imperial (Metric)

7 oz (200g) maize flour (cornmeal)
2 oz (50g) wholemeal flour
3-4 oz (75-100g) chopped almonds
3 eggs
2 oz (50g) butter
½ pint (¼ litre) water
2-3 oz (50-75g) honey
Dash of rum

1. Combine all the ingredients to form a smooth batter.
2. Heat the grease and waffle iron and spoon the mixture as required.
3. Cook at a medium heat for 5-7 minutes.

Note: Serve fresh with vanilla sauce!

Buckwheat

Buckwheat Casserole with Cheese

Serves 4 · P 16g, F 16g, C 40g, Cals 380

Imperial (Metric)

½ lb (¼ kilo) buckwheat
Approx. 1 pint (½ litre) vegetable stock
1 medium onion, chopped
1 red pepper, diced
2 tablespoonsful vegetable margarine
Sea salt and freshly ground black pepper
Basil, thyme and rosemary
1-2 cloves garlic, crushed
3 eggs, separated
4 oz (100g) grated cheese

1. Coarsely grind the buckwheat and allow to soak for 2-3 hours in the well seasoned stock.
2. Sauté the onion and pepper in the margarine, add the herbs and garlic and mix with the buckwheat.
3. Simmer for approximately 20-30 minutes, then add the egg yolks.
4. Whisk the egg whites until stiff, fold them into the buckwheat mixture and place it in a greased casserole.
5. Sprinkle with the cheese and bake for 35-40 minutes at 400°F/200°C (Gas Mark 6).

Buckwheat Porridge

Serves 4 · P 15g, F 4g, C 47g, Cals 285

Imperial (Metric)

1½-2 pints (¾-1 litre) skimmed milk
7 oz (200g) buckwheat, soaked
Pinch each of sea salt and raw cane sugar

1. Bring the milk to the boil and add the remaining ingredients.
2. Simmer for 20-25 minutes over a low heat.

Note: The porridge can be served with honey, dried fruit or fruit purée. If vegetable stock is used instead of milk, the buckwheat may be mixed with vegetables and cheese and baked in the oven.

7. Vegetable Omelette (page 55) with Frankfurt Dressing (page 121) and baked sage leaves

Courgette and Cheese Pasta Omelette

Serves 4   *Illustrated opposite*   P 20g, F 23g, C 55g, Cals 520

Imperial (Metric)

½ lb (¼ kilo) wholewheat pasta shells
3 pints (1½ litres) salted water
2 tablespoonsful vegetable margarine
2 medium onions, sliced
½ lb (¼ kilo) courgettes, sliced
Sea salt and freshly ground black pepper
4 eggs
¼ pint (150ml) milk
1-2 cloves garlic, crushed
Basil, thyme and rosemary
3-4 tablespoonsful coconut fat
4 tablespoonsful grated cheese

1. Cook the pasta for 10-15 minutes in boiling salted water. Set aside to drain.
2. Sauté the onions and courgettes in the hot margarine, simmer in a small amount of liquid for 5-10 minutes and season to taste.
3. Combine the eggs and milk and the garlic and herbs with the pasta and vegetables.
4. Cook 4 omelettes one after the other and sprinkle with cheese before serving.

8. Pasta and Mushroom Casserole (page 66) and Courgette and Cheese Pasta Omelette (page 65)

Pasta and Mushroom Casserole

Serves 4   *Illustrated opposite page 65*   P 18g, F 14g, C 70g, Cals 490

Imperial (Metric)

¾ lb (350g) wholewheat pasta shells
3-4 pints (1½-2 litres) water
2 tablespoonsful vegetable margarine
4 oz (100g) onions, chopped
½ lb (¼ kilo) mushrooms
Paprika
2 eggs
6 oz (150g) soured cream
Dash of milk
Mace
Sea salt and freshly ground black pepper

1. Cook the pasta in boiling water for 10-15 minutes, then allow to drain.
2. Heat the margarine and lightly sauté the onions and mushrooms.
3. Combine all the cooked ingredients and season well, then whisk together the remaining ingredients and pour the mixture over the casserole.
4. Bake for 25-30 minutes at 400°F/200°C (Gas Mark 6).

Spaghetti with Green Pepper

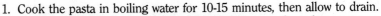

Serves 4   P 20g, F 17g, C 52g, Cals 459

Imperial (Metric)

½ lb (¼ kilo) wholewheat spaghetti
1 teaspoonful sea salt
1-2 green peppers
2 medium onions
2 tablespoonsful vegetable oil
¼ pint (150ml) milk
3 tablespoonsful cream
2 eggs
Sea salt and freshly ground black pepper
Nutmeg
4 oz (100g) grated cheese
1 bunch each of parsley and chives, chopped

1. Cook the spaghetti in salted water for 10-15 minutes.
2. Wash the peppers and dice them with the onions.
3. Sauté the vegetables and combine the remaining ingredients.
4. Drain the spaghetti and place it in a greased casserole.
5. Mix in the diced pepper and onion and pour over the egg and cheese mixture.
6. Bake at 425°F/220°C (Gas Mark 7) for approx. 15 minutes, then sprinkle with chives.

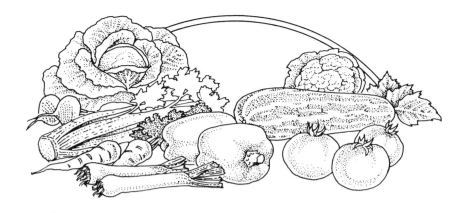

4.
VEGETABLE DISHES

In contrast to earlier times, all kinds of vegetables are now available throughout the year. What was once considered a luxury is now generally accepted: vegetables as well as fruit, have become part of the daily diet.

Vegetables not only taste good, they also contain nutrients. Fruit carbohydrates — glucose and fructose — are taken up directly into the blood-stream and are therefore good energy providers. Vegetable carbohydrates, however, take longer to digest and are not taken up so quickly by the blood-stream. This is particularly beneficial to diabetics and people who are overweight.

Cellulose, the fibrous matter in vegetables, is of considerable importance. Although it is indigestible it activates the wall of the intestine to promote effective digestion.

Vegetables, also have a fairly high vitamin and mineral content; in particular, the vitamins A, C and those of the B group, and potassium, calcium, phosphorus, iron and magnesium to name but a few.

The calorie content of fresh vegetables is minimal; one can eat plenty without risking excessive weight gain.

It must be remembered, of course, that overcooking vegetables should be avoided. Steaming, and cooking without any fat or water, are the best methods to use.

Cauliflower with Vinaigrette Dressing

Serves 4   P 10g, F 17g, C 9g, Cals 234

Imperial (Metric)

1 large cauliflower
Juice of ½ lemon
3 eggs

Dressing:
2 small onions
3 tablespoonsful each of chopped parsley and dill
3 tablespoonsful chopped chives
3 small gherkins
3-5 tablespoonsful fruit vinegar
5 tablespoonsful vegetable oil
3-4 tablespoonsful water
A little extra lemon juice
Sea salt and freshly ground black pepper
A little mustard
Pinch of raw cane sugar

1. Trim and wash the cauliflower then simmer it in salt water with the lemon juice for 20 minutes.
2. Boil the eggs for 10 minutes and, when cool, chop them into small pieces.
3. Combine the remaining ingredients to make a dressing and pour it over the strained cauliflower and pieces of egg.

Savoury Celeriac

Serves 4   P 2g, F 5g, C 12g, Cals 112

Imperial (Metric)

1½ lb (¾ kilo) celeriac
Juice of 1 lemon
2 tablespoonsful vegetable oil
1 onion, diced
1 vegetable stock cube, dissolved
Sea salt and freshly ground black pepper
Juice of 1 lemon
1 bunch of parsley

1. Peel and dice or slice the celeriac, then sprinkle it with lemon juice.
2. Heat the oil and sauté the onion, then add the celeriac.
3. Pour on the vegetable stock and simmer for 20 minutes.
4. Add salt, pepper and lemon juice to taste and sprinkle with parsley.

Celeriac Fritters

Serves 4 P 6g, F 9g, C 17g, Cals 194

Imperial (Metric)

Approx. 2 lb (1 kilo) celeriac
Sea salt and freshly ground black pepper
1 egg, beaten
2 tablespoonsful wheatgerm
2 tablespoonsful wholemeal breadcrumbs
3 tablespoonsful coconut fat

1. Cook the celeriac for about 45 minutes in salted water. Set aside to cool and then peel it.
2. Cut the celeriac into 4 or 8 slices and then halve them.
3. Season the celeriac and dip the pieces into the egg and then into the mixed wheatgerm and breadcrumbs.
4. Fry the slices in the hot coconut fat until both sides are golden.

Note: Serve with potato nests (page 96) and salad.

Baked Celery

Serves 4 P 12g, F 23g, C 14g, Cals 343

Imperial (Metric)

1½ lb (¾ kilo) celery, chopped
A little sea salt
1 pint (½ litre) water
4 tablespoonsful wholemeal flour
3 tablespoonsful vegetable oil
A little grated cheese
Sea salt and freshly ground black pepper
2 egg yolks
2 oz (50g) grated cheese for topping
1 tomato

1. Simmer the celery for about 8 minutes in the salted water, then set aside to drain.
2. Combine the flour with the oil in a saucepan, then add the stock from the celery and bring to the boil.
3. Add a little cheese, season to taste and stir in the beaten egg yolks to thicken.
4. Place the celery in a greased ovenproof dish and pour the sauce over the top.
5. Sprinkle on the remaining cheese and garnish with slices of tomato.
6. Bake for approximately 20 minutes at 425°F/220°C (Gas Mark 7).

Note: Serve with potatoes and parsley or Potato Nests (page 96).

Glazed Chestnuts

Serves 4　　　　　　　　　　　　　　　P 2g, F 5g, C 28g, Cals 168

Imperial (Metric)

1 lb (½ kilo) fresh chestnuts
Approx. 3 pints (1½ litres) vegetable stock
2 tablespoonsful butter

1. Cut a cross in the upper surface of the chestnuts and place them on a baking tray.
2. Bake for 10 minutes at 425°F/200°C (Gas Mark 7), then remove the skins.
3. Heat the vegetable stock and cook the chestnuts in it for 20-30 minutes. Drain well.
4. Melt the butter in a frying pan and toss the chestnuts in it whilst they are still hot.

Indian-Style Chicory

Serves 4　　　　　　　　　　　　　　　P 4g, F 10g, C 15g, Cals 163

Imperial (Metric)

1½-2 lb (¾-1 kilo) chicory
Juice of 1 lemon
Pinch of raw cane sugar
Sea salt and freshly ground black pepper
1 small onion, chopped
2 tablespoonsful vegetable oil
1 tablespoonful curry powder
1 tablespoonful wholemeal flour
¼ pint (150ml) water or vegetable stock
2 tablespoonsful cream
4 tablespoonsful desiccated coconut, toasted

1. Wash and halve the chicory.
2. Sprinkle with lemon juice and sugar, season and simmer in a small amount of water.
3. Sauté the onion and add the curry powder and flour.
4. Stir in the water or stock and bring to the boil.
5. Add the cream and season again.
6. Place the drained chicory on a serving dish, pour over the sauce and sprinkle with coconut.

Chicory au Gratin

Serves 4 P 4g, F 7g, C 4g, Cals 107

Imperial (Metric)

1½ lb (¾ kilo) chicory
Juice of ½ lemon
2 tablespoonsful white wine
1 tablespoonful vegetable oil
Pinch of sea salt
Pinch of raw cane sugar
2 oz (50g) grated cheese

1. Wash and halve the chicory.
2. Sprinkle with lemon juice and *sauté* in a large frying pan with a little water and wine. Simmer for 10-15 minutes.
3. Add the vegetable oil and seasoning.
4. Drain the chicory and place it in a greased casserole, then sprinkle with cheese.
5. Bake for approximately 10 minutes at 240°F/475°C (Gas Mark 9).

Savoury Courgettes

Serves 4 P 9g, F 15g, C 23g, Cals 241

Imperial (Metric)

2 lb (1 kilo) courgettes
Juice of 1 lemon
4 tablespoonsful vegetable oil
½ lb (¼ kilo) onions, diced
5 tablespoonsful white wine
Sea salt and freshly ground black pepper
1 clove garlic, crushed
2 tablespoonsful pine kernels

1. Halve the courgettes lengthways and chop them into pieces, then sprinkle on the lemon juice.
2. Heat the oil and sauté the onions, then add the courgettes and wine and a little water.
3. Simmer for 10 minutes and add the seasoning.
4. Sprinkle with the pine kernels.

Courgettes in Herby Tomato Sauce

Serves 4   P 3g, F 5g, C 15g, Cals 124

Imperial (Metric)

5 courgettes
2 small onions
4 tomatoes
2 tablespoonsful vegetable oil
Sea salt and freshly ground black pepper
1 tablespoonful tomato purée
1 tablespoonful yeast flakes
4 tablespoonsful white wine
Approx. ½ pint (¼ litre) vegetable or yeast extract stock
½ teaspoonful freshly chopped basil
1 tablespoonful freshly chopped dill

1. Chop the courgettes into thick slices.
2. Finely chop the onions and place the tomatoes in boiling water and then skin them.
3. Heat the vegetable oil and sauté the onions and courgettes.
4. Add the chopped tomatoes, seasoning, tomato purée and yeast flakes, wine and stock and simmer for 15-20 minutes.
5. Add basil and dill to taste.

Note: This is particularly good served with risotto.

Cucumber with Rice Stuffing

Serves 4   P 7g, F 9g, C 25g, Cals 220

Imperial (Metric)

2 cucumbers
3-4 oz (75-100g) brown rice
2 tablespoonsful vegetable oil
1 medium onion, chopped
4 oz (100g) mushrooms, chopped
2 oz (50g) vegetable pâté
1 egg
1 bunch of parsley, chopped
2 tablespoonsful tomato purée
Marjoram
Sea salt and freshly ground black pepper
1½ oz (40g) grated cheese

1. Remove the tips of the cucumber and halve it lengthways.
2. Scoop out the insides with a teaspoon, but do not remove all the fleshy part.
3. Blanche the cucumber in a little salt water for approximately 10 minutes.
4. Cook the rice in boiling water for 30 minutes and set it aside to drain.
5. Mix the rice with the sautéed onion and mushrooms, then add the pâté.
6. Mix in the egg, parsley, tomato purée and marjoram and season to taste.
7. Spoon the mixture into the cucumber halves.
8. Top with the cheese and bake in tin foil at 425°F/220°C (Gas Mark 7) for approximately 30 minutes.

Cucumber Savoury

Serves 4   P 2g, F 5g, C 5g, Cals 80

Imperial (Metric)

1 cucumber
2 tablespoonsful vegetable margarine
Sea salt
4 tablespoonsful tomato purée
2 cloves garlic, crushed
Marjoram
Thyme
Pinch of raw cane sugar

1. Peel the cucumber, halve it lengthways and cut into pieces 1 inch (2cm) wide.
2. Sauté the cucumber in the fat and season, then pour on a very little fluid and simmer for 15 minutes.
3. Mix the purée with the crushed garlic, herbs and sugar and combine with the cucumber.

Sautéed Fennel

Serves 4   P 5g, F 5g, C 22g, Cals 170

Imperial (Metric)

4-5 heads of fennel
2 tablespoonsful vegetable oil
A little water
¼ pint (150ml) white wine
Sea salt and freshly ground black pepper
Fennel leaves to garnish

1. Clean and halve the heads of fennel, then sauté them for 15-20 minutes in the oil, water and wine.
2. Season to taste and garnish with the chopped leaves.

Fennel and Tomato Savoury

Serves 4   P 3g, F 6g, C 23g, Cals 170

Imperial (Metric)

3-4 fennel
1 medium onion, quartered
2 tablespoonsful vegetable oil
4 tomatoes, skinned and chopped
Sea salt and freshly ground black pepper
Nutmeg

1. Wash and trim the fennel, removing the outer leaves (keep the leafy parts to use as a garnish).
2. Sauté the fennel and onion pieces in the oil and a small amount of water.
3. Add the tomatoes and sauté for another 5 minutes.
4. Season with salt, pepper and nutmeg and garnish with the chopped leaves.

Baked Kohlrabi

Serves 4   P 7g, F 10g, C 8g, Cals 156

Imperial (Metric)

4 medium kohlrabi
¼ pint (½ litre) milk
Sea salt and freshly ground black pepper
Nutmeg
Paprika
2-4 oz (50-100g) Parmesan cheese, grated
2 tablespoonsful vegetable margarine

1. Peel and dice the kohlrabi, then simmer it in a small amount of water for 10 minutes.
2. Place the kohlrabi in a heatproof casserole, combine the milk and seasoning and pour them over the top.
3. Sprinkle on the cheese and top with knobs of margarine, then bake until golden.

Note: Serve with all kinds of salad and creamed potatoes.

Buttered Kohlrabi

Serves 4   P 2g, F 3g, C 7g, Cals 112

Imperial (Metric)

4 medium kohlrabi
4 tablespoonsful butter
1 small onion, chopped
1 teaspoonful yeast extract dissolved in ¼ pint (150ml) water
Sea salt and freshly ground black pepper
Nutmeg
1 bunch of dill, chopped

1. Trim the kohlrabi (keep the leaves), then peel and slice it thinly.
2. Melt the butter and sauté the onions, then add the kohlrabi and yeast stock.
3. Simmer for 10 minutes then season to taste and sprinkle on the dill and finely chopped kohlrabi leaves.

Leeks in Cheese Sauce

Serves 4   P 7g, F 10g, C 13g, Cals 160

Imperial (Metric)

3 leeks
2 tablespoonsful vegetable oil
2 tablespoonsful wholemeal flour
½ pint (¼ litre) liquid, half milk, half vegetable stock
3 oz (75g) grated Emmental cheese
Pinch of raw cane sugar
Freshly ground black pepper
Nutmeg

1. Trim the leeks and chop them into 1½ inch (3cm) pieces, then simmer them in a small amount of water until just cooked.
2. Combine the oil and flour and pour on the liquid, then bring to the boil.
3. Add the grated cheese and seasoning and pour the sauce over the leeks.

Baked Leeks

Serves 4   P 10g, F 10g, C 18g, Cals 210

Imperial (Metric)

8 medium leeks
1 pint (½ litre) water
4 tablespoonsful vegetable oil
4-5 tablespoonsful wholemeal flour
Sea salt
A little wine
Freshly chopped parsley
2 egg yolks
2 oz (50g) grated cheese

1. Simmer the leeks in the liquid for 10-15 minutes.
2. Combine the oil with the flour, then add the leek water. Stir well and bring to the boil.
3. Season with the salt, wine and parsley and thicken with the egg yolks.
4. Place the leeks in a greased casserole, then pour over the sauce and sprinkle with cheese.
5. Bake for 15 to 20 minutes at 425°F/220°C (Gas Mark 7).

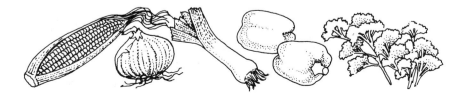

Sautéed Mushrooms

Serves 4   P 8g, F 8g, C 11g, Cals 141

Imperial (Metric)

Approx. 2 lb (1 kilo) mushrooms
Juice of 1 lemon
1 medium onion
3 tablespoonsful vegetable oil
Sea salt and freshly ground black pepper
Yeast extract
1 bunch of parsley

1. Trim the mushrooms (if necessary, remove any soft stalks) and wash them carefully.
2. Drain the mushrooms well and chop them coarsely. Sprinkle with lemon juice.
3. Peel and dice the onions and sauté them in the hot oil.
4. Add the mushrooms and simmer for approximately 15 minutes.
5. Season to taste and sprinkle with parsley.

Savoury Onions

Serves 4   P 4g, F 7g, C 21g, Cals 159

Imperial (Metric)

2 tablespoonsful vegetable margarine
1½ lb (¾ kilo) onions
½ pint (¼ litre) vegetable or yeast extract stock
Garlic powder
½ teaspoonful ground cumin
Pinch of raw cane sugar
1 teaspoonful cornflour
2 tablespoonsful cream
1 egg yolk
1-2 tablespoonsful chopped parsley

1. Heat the margarine and sauté the coarsely chopped or sliced onions, then add the stock.
2. Simmer for 10-15 minutes and add seasoning to taste.
3. Mix the cornflour with the cream and allow to boil briefly.
4. Add the cream mixture to the onions and use the egg yolk to thicken.
5. Sprinkle with parsley before serving.

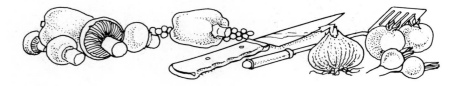

Peasant's Peas

Serves 4   P 13g, F 4g, C 57g, Cals 335

Imperial (Metric)

10 oz (300g) onions
10 oz (300g) carrots
1 lb (½ kilo) potatoes
2 tablespoonsful vegetable margarine
½ pint (¼ litre) vegetable stock
1 lb (½ kilo) peas, cooked
Sea salt and freshly ground black pepper
Pinch of raw cane sugar

1. Peel and dice the onions, carrots and potatoes, then sauté them in margarine.
2. Add the stock and simmer for 20 minutes.
3. Add the peas and seasoning.

Rice-Stuffed Peppers

Serves 4   P 4g, F 10g, C 28g, Cals 228

Imperial (Metric)

4 green peppers
4 oz (100g) brown rice
2 oz (50g) vegetable pâté
1 medium onion, diced
2 tablespoonsful vegetable oil
1 tablespoonful yeast flakes
Sea salt
A little vegetable stock

1. Remove the core and pith from the peppers, salt them inside and simmer them briefly.
2. Cook the rice in boiling water, drain and mix it with pâté.
3. Sauté the onion in the fat and add it to the rice with the seasoning.
4. Fill the peppers with the mixture and place them upright in a greased casserole.
5. Add a little liquid to the dish and cook for approx. 30 minutes or until cooked.
6. Serve with a tomato sauce.

Savoury Peppers

Serves 4   P 4g, F 5g, C 10g, Cals 95

Imperial (Metric)

5-6 green peppers
1 medium onion
2 tablespoonsful vegetable oil
¼ pint (150ml) water
4 tablespoonsful tomato purée
Sea salt and freshly ground black pepper
Pinch of raw cane sugar

1. Wash and finely slice the peppers.
2. Peel and dice the onions, then sauté them with the peppers in the oil.
3. Add the water and simmer for 15-20 minutes.
4. Add the remaining ingredients to taste.

Sauerkraut Casserole

Serves 4   P 20g, F 13g, C 30g, Cals 338

Imperial (Metric)

1 lb 4 oz (600g) Sauerkraut
14 oz (400g) potatoes
4 eggs
4 tablespoonsful milk
Sea salt and freshly ground black pepper
Nutmeg
Ground caraway
2 tomatoes
4 oz (100g) cheese
Chives to garnish

1. Place half the *Sauerkraut* in a heatproof dish.
2. Slice the potatoes thinly, add a little seasoning and layer them over the *Sauerkraut*. Place rest of *Sauerkraut* on top.
3. Combine the eggs, milk and seasoning and pour the mixture over the casserole.
4. Bake the casserole for 30-40 minutes at 425°F/220°C (Gas Mark 7).
5. Quarter the tomatoes and arrange them on the casserole with the cheese.
6. Bake for another 15 minutes and sprinkle with chives to garnish.

Sweet Sauerkraut Salad

Serves 4   P 2g, F 5g, C 12g, Cals 100

Imperial (Metric)

14 oz (400g) Sauerkraut
4 oz (100g) pineapple pieces
4 oz (100g) grapes

Dressing:
2-3 tablespoonsful pure pineapple juice
2 tablespoonsful white wine
2 tablespoonsful vegetable oil
A little sea salt and raw cane sugar

1. Chop up the *Sauerkraut,* place in a bowl and mix with the pineapple and grapes.
2. Combine the dressing ingredients and pour over the salad.

Savoury Sauerkraut Salad

Serves 4   P 2g, F 5g, C 9g, Cals 91

Imperial (Metric)

14 oz (400g) Sauerkraut
2 tomatoes
1 gherkin
1 small apple
2 tablespoonsful vegetable oil
1 teaspoonful apple concentrate
Sea salt
Ground caraway
A little onion salt

1. Chop up the *Sauerkraut* and place it in a bowl.
2. Dice the tomatoes, gherkin and apple and mix them in.
3. Pour over the oil and season with the remaining ingredients.
4. Arrange the salad on a bed of lettuce.

Note: This may be served with most main dishes and is particularly suitable for dieters.

Spinach and Potato Pudding

Serves 4   P 26g, F 18g, C 30g, Cals 395

Imperial (Metric)

1 lb (½ kilo) baked jacket potatoes
4 eggs, separated
Sea salt and freshly ground black pepper
Nutmeg
1 medium onion, chopped
2 tablespoonsful vegetable margarine
2 lb (1 kilo) spinach
4 oz (100g) grated cheese

1. Pass the potatoes through a sieve and mix in the egg yolks, seasoning and a little milk if needed.
2. Sauté the onion in the fat and add the spinach.
3. Combine the ingredients and the beaten egg whites, top with grated cheese and bake for 40-50 minutes at 400°F/200°C (Gas Mark 6).

Spinach Flan

Serves 4   P 15g, F 21g, C 22g, Cals 337

Imperial (Metric)

½ packet frozen wholemeal puff pastry
1½ lb (¾ kilo) spinach
2 tablespoonsful vegetable margarine
2 tablespoonsful wholemeal flour
¼ pint (150ml) milk
4 eggs
Sea salt and freshly ground black pepper
Nutmeg

1. Allow the pastry to thaw as directed on the packet.
2. Clean and trim the spinach and place it for 3-5 minutes in boiling salted water. Set aside to drain.
3. Heat the margarine and cook the flour briefly.
4. Stir in the milk, set aside to cool and mix in the eggs and seasoning.
5. Roll out the pastry and line a baking sheet with a border.
6. Spread the spinach on the pastry and top with the egg mixture.
7. Bake on the lowest rack for approximately 30 minutes at 425°F/220°C (Gas Mark 7).

Spinach-Stuffed Tomatoes

Serves 4   P 7g, F 6g, C 6g, Cals 106

Imperial (Metric)

8 medium tomatoes
½ lb (¼ kilo) spinach
1 bunch chervil
Sea salt and freshly ground black pepper
A little nutmeg
1 tablespoonful yeast flakes
2 slices Edam cheese
1 tablespoonful vegetable margarine

1. Scoop out the insides of the tomatoes and lightly salt them.
2. Blanch the spinach and chervil and season with the salt, pepper, nutmeg and yeast flakes.
3. Drain the mixture well and spoon into the tomatoes.
4. Sprinkle with pepper and top with a small piece of cheese.
5. Cover the tomatoes with a lid and place them in a greased heatproof dish.
6. Bake for 15 minutes at 400°F/200°C (Gas Mark 6).

Note: Tomatoes may also be filled with a soya tvp stuffing or a cheese and egg mixture.

Brussels Sprouts in White Sauce

Serves 4   P 9g, F 12g, C 16g, Cals 200

Imperial (Metric)

1½ lb (¾ kilo) Brussels sprouts
Salted water
Basic White Sauce (page 118)

1. Wash and trim the sprouts and cook them for 15 minutes in the water.
2. Mix the vegetables in the white sauce.

Turnip Patties

Serves 4   P 7g, F 7g, C 30g, Cals 255

Imperial (Metric)

14 oz (400g) turnips
10 oz (300g) potatoes
2 eggs
2 onions
2 oz (50g) wholemeal flour
Sea salt and freshly ground black pepper
A little mace
Coconut fat for frying

1. Grate the turnips and potatoes, leave to drain and then mix with the remaining ingredients.
2. Heat the fat in a frying pan and place small spoonsful of mixture in the pan. Serve with apple sauce.

Potato Dishes

The potato is a very important and nourishing food. It consists of two per cent valuable protein, twenty per cent starch, as well as fibre, minerals (particularly potassium) and vitamins (especially vitamin C).

When buying potatoes, make sure they have not sprouted; they should be firm and smooth-skinned. Packed potatoes should be removed from the bag as soon as possible to prevent rotting. The ideal storing temperature is between 4 and 6°C.

When cooking potatoes it is always best to leave the skins on if possible, otherwise a high proportion of the minerals and vitamins are lost in the cooking process.

Baked Potatoes

Serves 4   P 3g, F 4g, C 29g, Cals 166

Imperial (Metric)

8 medium potatoes
Sea salt
Caraway
2 tablespoonsful butter

1. Wash and scrub the potatoes, wrap them in tin foil and bake them for approximately 40 minutes at 475°F/240°C (Gas Mark 9).
2. Remove the foil and mark a cross in the top of each potato.
3. Season to taste and top with a knob of butter.

Quark and Potato Casserole

Serves 4　　　　　　　　　　　　　　　　　　　P 26g, F 16g, C 45g, Cals 450

Imperial (Metric)

1½ lb (¾ kilo) potatoes
A little sea salt and freshly ground black pepper
½ lb (¼ kilo) Quark
3 eggs
1 carton natural yogurt
2 tablespoonful wholemeal flour
Mace and marjoram
3-5 bunches of chives, chopped
½ lb (¼ kilo) soya tvp (previously soaked)
2 oz (50g) grated cheese (optional)

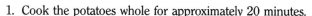

1. Cook the potatoes whole for approximately 20 minutes.
2. Slice the potatoes and place them in a greased casserole, then add seasoning.
3. Combine the Quark with the eggs, yogurt, flour and herbs.
4. Add the tvp (if necessary, dice it beforehand), and spoon the mixture onto the potatoes.
5. Top with cheese if liked and bake for approximately 30 minutes at 400°F/200°C (Gas Mark 6).

Potato and Fennel Casserole

Serves 4　　*Illustrated opposite page 96*　　　　　P 11g, F 7g, C 45g, Cals 290

Imperial (Metric)

3 heads of fennel
1 lb (½ kilo) potatoes
½ pint (¼ litre) liquid — ½ fennel stock, ½ milk
1 tablespoonful wholemeal flour
2 oz (50g) grated cheese
Sea salt and freshly ground black pepper
Pinch of raw cane sugar
Nutmeg
1 egg yolk
1 tablespoonful grated cheese to garnish

1. Simmer the fennel for approximately 15 minutes.
2. Cook the potatoes whole, then allow to cool and remove the skins.
3. Slice the fennel and potatoes and layer them in a greased casserole.
4. Bring the liquid to the boil and add the flour and cheese to thicken.
5. Add the seasoning and then stir in the egg when the mixture has cooled a little.
6. Pour the sauce over the vegetables and sprinkle with cheese, then bake for 20-30 minutes at 400°F/200°C (Gas Mark 6).

Caraway Potatoes

Serves 4   P 3g, F 5g, C 19g, Cals 172

Imperial (Metric)

1½ lb (¾ kilo) potatoes
A little ground caraway
Sea salt
4 tablespoonsful fresh linseed oil
2 tablespoonsful caraway seeds
Paprika

1. Wash and scrub the potatoes and slice them in half lengthways.
2. Season the cut sides with ground caraway and salt and place the potatoes cut-side down on an oiled baking sheet.
3. Brush the tops with oil and sprinkle with the caraway and paprika.
4. Bake for approximately 20 minutes at 425°F/220°C (Gas Mark 7) and serve as an accompaniment to savoury Quark dishes.

Béchamel Potatoes

Serves 4   P 6g, F 6g, C 30g, Cals 198

Imperial (Metric)

8-10 potatoes
2 tablespoonsful vegetable oil
2 tablespoonsful wholemeal flour
½ pint (¼ litre) milk
½ pint (¼ litre) vegetable stock
Sea salt and freshly ground black pepper
A little marjoram
2-3 tablespoonsful finely chopped dill

1. Boil the potatoes, then allow them to cool slightly before slicing them.
2. Place the oil and flour in a saucepan and pour on the milk and stock.
3. Bring to the boil stirring constantly and add plenty of seasoning.
4. Stir the potatoes into the sauce and re-heat them.
5. Season to taste again and stir in the dill just before serving.

94

Potato Goulash

Serves 4   P 8g, F 12g, C 50g, Cals 350

Imperial (Metric)

1½ lb (¾ kilo) potatoes
A little vegetable oil
3 medium onions, diced
½-1 pint (¼-½ litre) vegetable stock
1 teaspoonful paprika
Mace
Sea salt and freshly ground black pepper
4-5 tablespoonsful soured cream
1 bunch of chives, chopped

1. Dice the potatoes coarsely, then heat the oil and sauté the onions.
2. Add the potatoes to the pan and pour in the stock.
3. Cover the pan and simmer the vegetables for approximately 20 minutes, then season to taste.
4. Stir in the cream and sprinkle with chives.

Note: Serve with cold salads and pickles.

Potato Dumplings

Serves 4   P 7g, F 2g, C 53g, Cals 257

Imperial (Metric)

2 lb (1 kilo) potatoes
¼ pint (150ml) milk
Sea salt
Nutmeg
1 tablespoonful wholemeal flour
2 tablespoonsful wheatgerm
1 bunch of parsley
1 bunch of chives

1. Boil half of the potatoes and meanwhile peel and grate the rest and simmer them in the warm milk.
2. Mash the boiled potatoes and mix in the milk and potato mixture.
3. Add the salt, nutmeg, flour and wheatgerm as well as the chopped parsley and chives.
4. Shape the mixture into 8 small dumplings and simmer them in plenty of salted water for approximately 20 minutes.

Note: It is a good idea to try cooking one dumpling separately, and then add a little more flour to the mixture if the dumpling falls apart.

Potato Nests

Serves 4   P 9g, F 6g, C 29g, Cals 208

Imperial (Metric)

1½ lb (¾ kilo) potatoes
1 egg
¼ pint (150ml) milk
Sea salt
Nutmeg

Filling:
2 eggs, separated
3-4 oz (75-100g) grated cheese
Sea salt and freshly ground black pepper

1. Boil and mash the potatoes and mix in the egg and warm milk. Season to taste.
2. Pipe the stiff potato mixture onto an oiled baking sheet to form small nest shapes.
3. Beat the egg whites and combine them with the yolks, cheese and seasoning, then spoon this mixture into the nests.
4. Bake for 10-15 minutes at 475°F/240°C (Gas Mark 9).

Potato Pancakes with Bran

Serves 4   *Illustrated opposite*   P 8g, F 11g, C 41g, Cals 292

Imperial (Metric)

1½ lb (¾ kilo) potatoes
1 medium onion
2 eggs
1 tablespoonful wholemeal flour
1 tablespoonful bran
Sea salt
Nutmeg
3-4 tablespoonsful vegetable oil

1. Peel and grate the potatoes and set them aside to drain a while.
2. Grate the onion and mix it with the potatoes adding the flour, bran and seasoning.
3. Heat the oil in a frying pan and spoon in enough of the mixture to make a pancake.

Note: Serve with apple sauce, fruit purée or salad.

9.   Potato and Fennel Casserole (page 93), Potato Soup (page 35) and
     Potato Pancakes (page 96)

Potatoes with Cream Cheese

Serves 4   P 14g, F 9g, C 38g, Cals 297

Imperial (Metric)

1½ lb (¾ kilo) baking potatoes
5 oz (125g) grated cheese
2½ oz (65g) cream cheese
1 bunch each of dill, chives and parsley
Sea salt and freshly ground black pepper
1 clove of garlic
¼-½ pint (150-250ml) well seasoned vegetable stock

1. Boil the potatoes whole for about 30 minutes, then halve them lengthways.
2. Place the potatoes cut-side uppermost in an ovenproof dish.
3. Mix the cheeses and chopped herbs and add the seasoning.
4. Pour a little stock around the base of the potatoes and top each one with some of the cheese mixture.
5. Bake for approximately 15 minutes at 425°F/220°C (Gas Mark 7).

Note: Serve with lettuce salad, tomatoes or watercress.

10.   Picnic salads

5.
SALADS

Salads and raw vegetables have the great advantage of being refreshing, light, and since they need no cooking, high in vitamins and minerals. They are also good for the digestive system as they are high-fibre foods.

Many people do not think to serve vegetables raw, on the grounds that too much work is involved. In fact salad preparation is not time-consuming, especially if you have modern kitchen gadgets to help you. All kinds of vegetables are suitable for salads providing they are fresh and in perfect condition. Some vegetables are good in combination with certain fruits.

As salad seasoners, try to use fresh herbs instead of salt and replace mayonnaise with yogurt, Quark, vegetable oils and lemon juice. Dressings can be varied each time by adding tomato purée, ketchup, horseradish, onions, garlic, mustard or a pinch of raw cane sugar and a drop of apple concentrate.

Salads are suitable for all mealtimes; serve as a starter instead of soup or as a side dish to a main meal on hot summer days. Salads also make ideal snacks or light supper dishes.

Salad Combinations

Carrots	— with cress, celery or apple
Celery	— with apple, carrots or pears and nuts
Cauliflower	— with banana
Sauerkraut	— with pineapple, apple, cucumber or onions
Beetroot	— with apple or a little pure blackcurrant juice
Chicory (Endive)	— with mandarins, oranges, grapefruit or cucumber
Cucumber	— with cress, radishes, tomatoes, green pepper or lettuce
Tomatoes	— with cress, green pepper, cucumber or lettuce. (Add a little crumbled sheep's cheese to vary this salad.)
Radishes	— with cress, lettuce, chicory (endive) and cucumber

Plain Green Salad

Serves 4   P 2g, F 7g, C 4g, Cals 80

Imperial (Metric)

1 large or 2 small heads lettuce

Dressing:
1 carton natural yogurt
2 tablespoonsful sunflower oil
Juice of 1 lemon
Sea salt and freshly ground black pepper
1 tablespoonful apple concentrate
Fresh herbs

1. Prepare the lettuce by washing, tearing into pieces and drying well.
2. For the dressing, combine all the ingredients and season to taste.

Note: Add herbs according to the season, freshly chopped. Pour on the dressing just before serving. This dressing will go well with most leafy salads, and also with root vegetables served raw.

Endive Salad

Serves 4   P 1g, F 10g, C 5g, Cals 115

Imperial (Metric)

1 head of endive
Small amount of pickled vegetables
2 tomatoes
4 tablespoonsful vegetable oil
Vinegar from pickled vegetables
Sea salt and freshly ground black pepper

1. Prepare the endive and cut into strips.
2. If necessary, chop the pickled vegetables into small pieces, and dice the tomato.
3. Combine the remaining ingredients, mix with the salad and garnish with the tomatoes.

Turnip Salad

Serves 4   P 1g, F 8g, C 15g, Cals 130

Imperial (Metric)

Approx. 1 lb (½ kilo) turnips
2-3 slices of pineapple
A little pure pineapple juice
A little lemon juice
2-3 tablespoonsful vegetable oil
A little sea salt

1. Peel and finely grate the turnips.
2. Chop the pineapple and mix it in with the other ingredients.

Red Cabbage Salad
with Cheese Dressing

Serves 4   P 8g, F 7g, C 7g, Cals 125

Imperial (Metric)

1 small red cabbage

Dressing:
4 oz (100g) sheep's cheese
1 carton natural yogurt
1 clove garlic
A little sea salt and lemon juice

1. Finely chop the cabbage and sieve the cheese.
2. Mix in the yogurt, garlic, salt and lemon juice to taste.

Sweet Cabbage Salad

Serves 4   P 2g, F 13g, C 7g, Cals 155

Imperial (Metric)

½ white cabbage

Dressing:
3 tablespoonsful cream
1 teaspoonful honey
Juice of 1 lemon
A little sea salt
1-2 tablespoonsful coarsely chopped hazelnuts

1. Finely chop the cabbage.
2. Combine the remaining ingredients except for the nuts and mix in the cabbage.
3. Allow the salad to stand for 30 minutes, then garnish with the chopped nuts.

Onion and Apple Salad

Serves 4   P 3g, F 1g, C 12g, Cals 65

Imperial (Metric)

1 large onion
2 medium apples (red if possible)
1 carton natural yogurt
Juice of ½ lemon
Pinch of raw cane sugar
A little sea salt
Finely chopped parsley

1. Peel and halve the onion, then finely slice it.
2. Slice the apples finely.
3. Make a dressing with the remaining ingredients and mix in the onion and apples.

Egg Salad

Serves 1   P 17g, F 17g, C 21g, Cals 319

Imperial (Metric)

2 hard-boiled eggs
1 tomato
1 gherkin

Dressing:
1 tablespoonful soured cream
A little fruit vinegar
Sea salt and freshly ground black pepper
Fresh herbs

1. Slice the eggs, tomato and gherkin.
2. Mix the dressing ingredients and combine with the salad.

Note: Boil the eggs the previous evening, and prepare the dressing, but only combine the two just before serving.

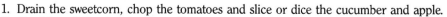

Filling, Hearty Salads

Sweetcorn Salad

Serves 4   P 4g, F 5g, C 13g, Cals 110

Imperial (Metric)

1 small tin sweetcorn
2 tomatoes
½ cucumber
1 apple

Dressing:
2 tablespoonsful vegetable oil
2 tablespoonsful fruit vinegar
Sea salt and freshly ground black pepper
Chopped chives

1. Drain the sweetcorn, chop the tomatoes and slice or dice the cucumber and apple.
2. Combine all the dressing ingredients.
3. Mix the dressing with the salad vegetables.

Pasta Salad

Serves 1   P 8g, F 12g, C 48g, Cals 335

Imperial (Metric)

2 oz (50g) wholewheat pasta
1 tablespoonful cooked peas
1 tablespoonful chopped mushrooms
½ apple, chopped

Dressing:
1 tablespoonful vegetable oil
A little fruit vinegar
Sea salt and freshly ground black pepper
A little apple concentrate
Chopped chives

1. Cook the pasta in salted water until just soft, then mix in the peas, mushrooms and apple.
2. Pour over the dressing.

Note: This salad can be prepared the previous evening but must be stored in a cool place.

Wholewheat Pasta Salad with Mushrooms

Serves 4   P 8g, F 10g, C 41g, Cals 300

Imperial (Metric)

7 oz (200g) wholewheat pasta shells, cooked
½ lb (¼ kilo) button mushrooms
1 medium onion, sliced
1 carton soured cream
1 teaspoonful mustard
Sea salt and freshly ground black pepper
Pinch of raw cane sugar
Garlic powder
Lemon juice
Chopped chives

1. Place the pasta, mushrooms and onion in a bowl.
2. Combine the remaining ingredients to make a dressing and mix in with the salad.

Piquant Rice Salad

Serves 4   P 10g, F 8g, C 30g, Cals 240

Imperial (Metric)

6 oz (150g) brown rice
Sea salt
½ cucumber, diced
2 tomatoes, diced
1 green pepper, diced
1 red pepper, diced

Dressing:
4 tablespoonsful vegetable oil
2-3 tablespoonsful fruit vinegar
3-4 tablespoonsful water
Sea salt and freshly ground black pepper
Pinch of raw cane sugar
Paprika

1. Cook the rice in boiling salted water for 30-35 minutes, drain and set aside to cool.
2. Add the vegetables to the rice.
3. Combine the dressing ingredients and mix in the salad. Leave to stand and add more seasoning if necessary.

Cheese Salad

Serves 4   P 11g, F 21g, C 15g, Cals 304

Imperial (Metric)

6 oz (150g) Gouda or Emmental cheese
7 oz (200g) green grapes
4 oz (100g) black grapes
2 oz (50g) walnuts
2 tablespoonsful vegetable oil
Juice of 1-2 lemons
Pinch of raw cane sugar
Sea salt and freshly ground black pepper

1. Slice the cheese, then halve the grapes and remove the pips.
2. Chop the nuts coarsely.
3. Combine all the ingredients carefully.

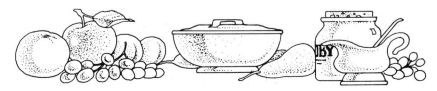

Barley Salad

Serves 4   P 6g, F 4g, C 35g, Cals 215

Imperial (Metric)

6 oz (150g) barley corn
2 pints (1 litre) water
1 vegetable stock cube
1 bay leaf
Sea salt
3 tomatoes
2 shallots

Dressing:
6 oz (150g) soured cream
Pinch of raw cane sugar
Pinch of sea salt
Garlic powder
Freshly ground black pepper
A little mustard
Cress to garnish

1. Soak the barley overnight in the water and then simmer it over a low heat in the same water, with the stock cube, bay leaf and salt.
2. Scoop the insides out of the tomatoes and dice them, then finely slice the shallots.
3. Combine all the dressing ingredients and then mix in the strained barley, tomatoes and shallots.
4. Leave to stand and garnish with cress.

Soya Bean Sprout Salad

Serves 4   P 3g, F 10g, C 12g, Cals 155

Imperial (Metric)

Approx. 10 oz (300g) soya bean shoots (tinned or sprouted at home)
Approx. 3 oz (75g) mung beans (sprouted for 4-5 days)
4 tablespoonsful sunflower oil
Juice of ½ lemon
Pinch of raw cane sugar
Sea salt
1 tablespoonful soya sauce
Pinch of ginger
1 small onion, diced
1 tomato, chopped

1. Blanch the bean shoots for 2-3 minutes and set aside to cool.
2. Prepare a dressing with the remaining ingredients, mix in the bean sprouts and garnish with tomato.

11.   Spinach Salad (page 103) and Tomato Salad (page 98)

Sprouted Wheat Salad

Serves 4   P 3g, F 10g, C 20g, Cals 200

Imperial (Metric)

Approx. 4 oz (100g) wheat
2 small beetroot
4 tablespoonsful sunflower oil
1 teaspoonful horseradish
Pinch of raw cane sugar
Sea salt
Juice of 1-2 lemons
A little cumin powder (optional)

1. Sprout the wheat grains over 3 days, rinsing each day.
2. Peel and finely grate the beetroot.
3. Prepare a dressing with the remaining ingredients.
4. Combine all the ingredients and leave to stand for about 30 minutes before serving.

Note: Sprouted wheat also combines well with cauliflower, celery and carrot salads as well as lettuce.

Wheat Salad with Green Pepper and Tomato

Serves 4   *Illustrated opposite page 49*   P 5g, F 10g, C 25g, Cals 225

Imperial (Metric)

5-6 oz (125-150g) wheat, soaked for 8-10 hours
1 green pepper
2 medium tomatoes or ½ cucumber
1 bunch of chives
4 tablespoonsful sunflower oil
Juice of 1-2 lemons
2 cloves garlic
A little mustard
Sea salt and freshly ground black pepper
Pinch of raw cane sugar

1. Simmer the wheat for 50-60 minutes then leave to cool.
2. Dice the green pepper and tomatoes or cucumber and finely chop the chives.
3. Make a dressing with the remaining ingredients and mix in the wheat mixture.
4. Leave to stand for about an hour before serving.

12.   Dandelion Salad (page 116)

Salads with Herbs

The following plants grow wild and are often thought of as weeds; they do, however, taste delicious and provide all sorts of valuable vitamins and minerals for the body.

Nettles — act as a diuretic and aids blood formation in the body.
Watercress — has a very high mineral and vitamin C content.
Coltsfoot — the main active ingredient in this plant are mucilage substances which have a beneficial effect against colds and also in cases of stomach upsets.
Dandelion — acts as a diuretic.
Ribwort — has a high mucilage content and is therefore used against chest complaints.
Sorrel — makes an ideal spring salad; rich in vitamin C.

Note: These plants should only be collected from areas which are free from traffic, and are best picked early in the day.

Watercress Salad

Serves 4   P 2g, F 12g, C 5g, Cals 120

Imperial (Metric)

7 oz (200g) watercress

Dressing:
3-4 tablespoonsful walnut oil
Juice of ½ lemon
A little mustard
½ teaspoonful honey
Sea salt
10 walnut halves

1. Wash the watercress.
2. Combine the dressing ingredients and mix with the watercress.
3. Roughly chop the walnuts and sprinkle them over the salad.

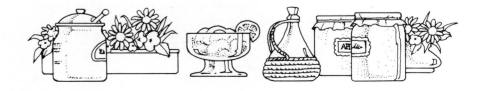

Sweet Sorrel Salad

Serves 4   P 2g, F 10g, C 4g, Cals 112

Imperial (Metric)

½ lb (¼ kilo) sorrel
¼ pint (150ml) cream
1 teaspoonful honey
Juice of 1 lemon
Pinch of sea salt

1. Prepare the sorrel by washing and trimming.
2. Prepare the dressing by combining the remaining ingredients and mix in the sorrel.

Piquant Sorrel Salad

Serves 4   P 3g, F 10g, C 2g, Cals 94

Imperial (Metric)

½ lb (¼ kilo) sorrel
Yolks of 2 hard-boiled eggs
A little mustard
2 tablespoonsful sunflower oil
2 tablespoonsful fruit vinegar
Sea salt and freshly ground black pepper
½ onion, finely chopped

1. Prepare the sorrel by washing and trimming.
2. Mash the egg yolks and mix in the remaining ingredients.
3. Toss the sorrel in the dressing.

7.
DESSERTS

A dessert should round off a meal both tastily and nutritionally. Neither need it always be sweet, for many people like to savour the taste of the main dish; the French, for example, often prefer cheese or fresh fruit as a dessert.

Desserts best avoided are those that contain a lot of sugar or fat and thus calories. Wholefood sweets may be made from milk, Quark, yogurt, vegetables, unsweetened fruit juices, honey and nuts. These are not only good for slimming, but also provide essential nutrients as well as energy.

Milk and Quark Desserts

Orange Quark

Serves 4   P 11g, F 1g, C 15g, Cals 113

Imperial (Metric)

½ lb (¼ kilo) Quark
⅓ pint (200ml) apple juice
Juice of 1 lemon
1 tablespoonful honey
1 orange

1. Combine the Quark, apple and lemon juices with the honey (if possible, with an electric mixer).
2. Peel the orange and cut it into even-sized pieces, using some to mix with the Quark and saving some as garnish.

Fruit Salad with Buttermilk

Serves 4   P 4g, F 4g, C 29g, Cals 172

Imperial (Metric)

6 oz (150g) of each fruit according to season e.g., apples, oranges, pears, bananas
1-2 tablespoonsful pear concentrate
Juice of 1 lemon
½ pint (¼ litre) buttermilk
2 tablespoonsful chopped nuts

1. If necessary, peel the fruit and mix it with the pear concentrate and lemon juice.
2. Divide the fruit into 4 dishes and pour on the buttermilk, then decorate with nuts.

Date Quark

Serves 4   P 15g, F 10g, C 28g, Cals 254

Imperial (Metric)

½ lb (¼ kilo) Quark
⅓ pint (200ml) milk
1 tablespoonful honey
5 oz (125g) dates
2 oz (50g) almonds

1. Blend the Quark with the milk and honey.
2. Finely chop the dates and almonds and mix them in.
3. Garnish each portion with a little chopped date.

Strawberry Quark

Serves 4   P 13g, F 2g, C 15g, Cals 145

Imperial (Metric)

½ lb (¼ kilo) Quark
⅓ pint (200ml) milk
Juice of 1 lemon
½ lb (¼ kilo) strawberries, finely chopped
1-2 tablespoonsful chopped nuts

1. Blend the Quark with the milk and lemon juice.
2. Fold in the strawberries or blend them in a liquidizer.
3. Garnish each portion with a sprinkling of nuts.

Hazelnut Quark

Serves 4   P 14g, F 10g, C 11g, Cals 200

Imperial (Metric)

½ lb (¼ kilo) Quark
⅓ pint (200ml) milk
2 tablespoonsful honey
Few drops pure vanilla essence
Juice of 1 lemon
3 tablespoonsful hazelnut purée
2 tablespoonsful chopped nuts

1. Blend all the ingredients together except for the chopped nuts.
2. Fold in the chopped nuts.

Creamy Quark with Peaches

Serves 4   P 9g, F 2g, C 20g, Cals 140

Imperial (Metric)

5 oz (125g) Quark
½ pint (¼ litre) milk
Few drops of pure vanilla essence
4 peach halves, skinned
2 tablespoonful chopped nuts

1. Blend the Quark with the milk and vanilla and spoon the mixture into glass dishes.
2. Place the peach halves in the middle of the Quark mixture and decorate the edges with chopped nuts.

Creamy Quark with Pears

Serves 4   P 7g, F 0g, C 17g, Cals 100

Imperial (Metric)

4 pears
A little white wine
1 tablespoonful maple syrup
Rind of lemon
½ stick cinnamon
3 cloves
6 oz (150g) Quark
A little milk
Few drops pure vanilla essence
Few drops of chopped peach

1. Peel the pears and simmer them while still whole covered with the wine, lemon rind, cinnamon and cloves, for about 10 minutes.
2. Allow the pears to cool in the wine mixture.
3. To serve, place the pears in a deep dish and cover with the blended Quark, milk and vanilla essence, then garnish with the peach.

Banana Quark with Cinnamon

Serves 4   P 10g, F 4g, C 16g, Cals 133

Imperial (Metric)

⅓ pint (200ml) milk
1-2 tablespoonful honey
1 medium banana
1 teaspoonful cinnamon
½ lb (¼ kilo) Quark

1. Blend the milk, honey, banana and cinnamon and then stir in the Quark.

Fruity Desserts

Baked Bananas

Serves 4   P 2g, F 1g, C 30g, Cals 136

Imperial (Metric)

4 bananas
4 squares of tin foil
Juice of 2 lemons
A little wine
2 tablespoonsful honey
2 tablespoonsful chopped nuts

1. Peel the bananas and place each one on a piece of tin foil.
2. Roll up the foil on each side, then pour on a little lemon juice and wine onto each banana — the liquid should not leak out from around the bananas.
3. Dot the bananas with honey and sprinkle with the chopped nuts, then close the foil at the top and bake for approximately 40 minutes at 450°F/230°C (Gas Mark 8).

Baked Apples with Rosehips

Serves 4   P 3g, F 1g, C 17g, Cals 90

Imperial (Metric)

4 medium apples
2 tablespoonsful rosehip purée
2 tablespoonsful Quark
1-2 egg yolks
A little cinnamon
1 teaspoonful honey
Juice of ½ lemon — optional

1. Remove the apple cores.
2. Combine the remaining ingredients and spoon the mixture into the apples until they are packed full.
3. Bake for 20-30 minutes at 425°F/220°C (Gas Mark 7).

Note: Chopped nuts, sesame seeds or raisins may also be added to this stuffing mixture.

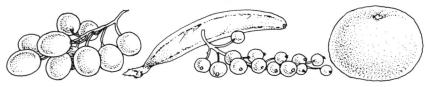

Mixed Fruit Salad

Serves 4   P 2g, F 8g, C 27g, Cals 197

Imperial (Metric)

1¼ lb (600g) seasonal fruit
Juice of 2 lemons
1 oz (25g) raisins
2 oz (50g) nuts
Dash of Kirsch

1. Prepare and chop the fruit.
2. Sprinkle the lemon juice over the fruit.
3. Mix in the raisins and nuts and pour on the Kirsch.

Grape and Banana Salad

Serves 4   P 2g, F 5g, C 18g, Cals 143

Imperial (Metric)

1 lb (½ kilo) grapes
1 small banana
1 tablespoonful Kirsch
1½ oz (40g) chopped hazelnuts

1. Wash and halve the grapes and remove the pips.
2. Peel and chop the bananas and add Kirsch.
3. Sprinkle with hazelnuts.

Rote Grütze

Serves 8   *Illustrated opposite*   P 2g, F 0g, C 78g, Cals 315

Imperial (Metric)

1½ lb (¾ kilo) black cherries, stoned
½ lb (¼ kilo) each of redcurrants, blackcurrants and raspberries, fresh or deep-frozen
¼ pint (150ml) raspberry syrup
6 oz (150g) cornflour
6 oz (150g) red cherries, stoned

1. Simmer the black cherries, redcurrants, blackcurrants and raspberries in a little water then purée them through a sieve.

128   13.   Rote Grüze (page 128)

2. Add enough water to the fruit to make up 3 pints (1½ litres), then stir in the raspberry syrup and bring to the boil.
3. Mix the cornflour with a little water and stir it into the fruit.
4. Add the red cherries and bring the fruit back to the boil.
5. Allow the mixture to cool and then refrigerate it. Serve with whipped cream or milk.

Mixed Currant Jelly

Serves 4   P 4g, F 9g, C 32g, Cals 235

Imperial (Metric)

Approx. 4 oz (100g) kibbled rye
2 pints (1 litre) water
Pinch of sea salt
Pinch of raw cane sugar
½ lb (¼ kilo) red and blackcurrants
A little blackcurrant syrup
Juice of ½ lemon
¼ pint (150ml) cream

1. Simmer the rye in the water with the salt and sugar for 20-30 minutes.
2. Allow to cool, then add the currants.
3. Add the syrup and lemon juice, pour into deep dishes and serve with cream.

Apple Fool

Serves 4   P 1g, F 11g, C 22g, Cals 162

Imperial (Metric)

1¼ lb (600g) apple purée
½ teaspoonful cinnamon
Juice of 1 lemon
¼ pint (150ml) cream
2 tablespoonsful grated chocolate

1. Mix the apple with the cinnamon and lemon juice.
2. Fold in the whipped cream and decorate with the chocolate.

14.   A selection of wholemeal breads

Sweet Apple Salad

Serves 4   P 2g, F 4g, C 28g, Cals 162

Imperial (Metric)

4 medium apples
Juice of 1 lemon
1 teaspoonful maple syrup or to taste
2 tablespoonsful chopped almonds
2 oz (50g) raisins, soaked

1. Chop the apples and sprinkle them with lemon juice.
2. If necessary, add a little maple syrup to the apples, then stir in the almonds and raisins.

Peppered Strawberries

Serves 4   P 2g, F 9g, C 10g, Cals 139

Imperial (Metric)

1 lb (½ kilo) strawberries
Freshly ground black pepper
¼ pint (150ml) cream, chilled

1. Wash the strawberries and arrange them in 4 dishes.
2. Sprinkle the fruit with pepper and top with cream.

Quark-Filled Pancakes

Serves 4   *Illustrated opposite page 16*   P 19g, F 24g, C 4g, Cals 468

Imperial (Metric)

5 oz (125g) wholemeal flour
½ pint (¼ litre) milk
Sea salt
1 tablespoonful honey
2 eggs
2 tablespoonsful vegetable oil

Filling:
½ lb (¼ kilo) Quark
1 tablespoonful honey
2 egg yolks
A little rum
2 oz (50g) raisins
2 tablespoonsful butter

1. Combine all the pancake ingredients and cook scoopsful of the mixture in the hot vegetable oil.
2. Blend the Quark with the honey, eggs and rum then stir in the raisins.
3. Allow the pancakes to cool then spread them quickly with the Quark mixture and roll up the pancakes.
4. Set the pancakes out in a casserole and dot them with butter, then bake them for 20 minutes at 400°F/200°C (Gas Mark 6).

Note: Since this recipe is high in calories it is best served after a light main course such as a salad or a soup.

Apple Meringue

Serves 4   P 10, F 14g, C 24g, Cals 262

Imperial (Metric)

1 lb (½ kilo) apples
Juice of 2 lemons
4 eggs, separated
2 oz (50g) hazelnuts, ground
2-3 tablespoonsful fructose

1. Peel and core the apples and simmer them with the lemon juice until almost cooked, then place them in a greased casserole.
2. Cream the egg yolks with the hazelnuts and fructose and fold in the stiffly beaten egg whites.
3. Spoon the meringue-type mixture over the apples and bake for approximately 20 minutes at 350°F/180°C (Gas Mark 4).

Note: This dish is ideal for diabetics.

Honey Custards

Serves 4   P 10g, F 12g, C 13g, Cals 200

Imperial (Metric)

½ pint (¼ litre) milk
2 tablespoonsful cream
3-4 tablespoonsful honey
4 eggs
A little pure vanilla essence

1. Combine all the ingredients and pour the mixture into four small dishes or cups (grease them beforehand).
2. Bake in a baking tin with a little water surrounding the dishes for 1 hour at 225°F/110°C (Gas Mark ¼) or until the custards have set.

Sweet Quark Dumplings

Serves 4   P 11g, F 5g, C 38g, Cals 260

Imperial (Metric)

6 oz (50g) Quark
1 egg
1 tablespoonful vegetable oil
6 oz (150g) kibbled wheat
2-3 oz (50-75g) raisins
2 tablespoonsful honey
Pinch of sea salt

1. Combine all the ingredients and simmer for 10 minutes.
2. Form little dumplings from the mixture and cook them in simmering water for 10-15 minutes.

Note: These are particularly good served with stewed berries.

Sweet Wholemeal Dumplings

Serves 4   P 8g, F 16g, C 40g, Cals 390

Imperial (Metric)

7 oz (200g) wholemeal flour
2-3 eggs
¼ pint (150ml) milk or water
½ teaspoonful sea salt
1-2 tablespoonsful honey
2 oz (50g) hazelnuts, coarsely chopped
1 tablespoonful coconut fat

1. Combine the flour, egg yolks, milk or water, salt, honey and nuts and fold in the stiffly beaten egg whites.
2. Heat the fat in a frying pan and cook scoopsful of the mixture on both sides.

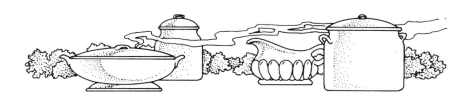

8.
BREADS, CAKES AND PASTRIES

Cereal crops in general are an economic and natural form of nourishment. The inside of the grain consists mainly of starch, whereas the important minerals, vitamins and fibre are found in the germ and outerlayers. The advantages of eating whole grains are well-known, both in terms of health and of satisfying the appetite.

Tips for Baking with Wholemeal Flour

★ If you are grinding your own flour, the grain should never be too fresh and it must always be stored in a dry place; above all this prevents the mill blades becoming clogged!

★ When making a wholemeal dough, roughly one third extra liquid is required as opposed to baking with white flour. The outer layers of the grain absorb more liquid than refined flour and the dough would otherwise be too crumbly.

★ Also, the amount of raising agent should be increased by one third — this makes the dough spongier, it does not retain as much moisture and is therefore easier to digest.

★ The dough should be set aside for at least 1 hour before baking so that it can rise well.

★ Two types of raising agent are to be preferred: yeast (either fresh or dried) and sour-dough starter which can be made at home, but which should be used in combination with a small amount of yeast.

★ Thorough kneading and proving is essential in order to make the dough soft.

★ In order to prevent a hard crust forming on the bread or rolls, sprinkle or brush a little lukewarm water on the dough before baking, moisten the baking tray and place a cupful of water in the oven with the bread.

★ Brush the bread with a little water or beer once it has cooked and is still hot; this will give it an attractive glaze.

Sour-Dough Starter for Granary Bread

Enough for 2 loaves

Imperial (Metric)

Approx. 4 oz (100g) kibbled rye
1 teaspoonful ground caraway seeds
1 teaspoonful ground fennel seeds
1 tablespoonful raw cane sugar
A little lukewarm buttermilk

1. Mix all the ingredients together to a thick paste.
2. Dust the top with wholemeal flour so that the dough does not dry out too much; cover the bowl with a tea-towel and set aside in a warm, draught-free spot.
3. Knead the starter each day, if necessary adding a little lukewarm water.

Note: The leavening process takes 2-3 days.

Granary Bread with Sour-Dough Starter

Imperial (Metric)

14 oz (400g) wholemeal flour
½ lb (¼ kilo) kibbled rye
½ pint (¼ litre) lukewarm milk
2 oz (50g) dried yeast
1 teaspoonful raw cane sugar
½ quantity Sour-Dough Starter (above)
2-3 teaspoonsful sea salt
1 teaspoonful ground caraway seeds
½ teaspoonful coriander, sesame or poppy seeds

1. Mix together the flour and rye in a bowl and make a well in the centre.
2. Mix a little of the milk with the yeast and sugar and add this to the flour.
3. Cover thebowl with a tea-towel and set aside for about 15 minutes.
4. Add the remaining milk, the sour-dough, salt, caraway and coriander and combine thoroughly, kneading with the hands or an electric mixer.
5. Shape the dough into a loaf and set aside for about 30 minutes.
6. Brush with lukewarm milk and sprinkle with sesame or poppy seeds.
7. Bake for about 50 minutes in a pre-heated oven at 425°F/220°C (Gas Mark 7).

Note: Leave a cupful of water in the oven with the bread.

Mixed Grain Bread

Imperial (Metric)

½ lb (¼ kilo) wholemeal flour
½ lb (¼ kilo) wholemeal rye flour
6 oz (150g) kibbled wheat
Approx ⅔ pint (400ml) lukewarm water
2 oz (50g) dried yeast
1 teaspoonful raw cane sugar
3-4 teaspoonsful sea salt
Extra kibbled wheat

1. Mix together the flours and the kibbled wheat in a bowl and make a well in the centre.
2. Mix a little of the water with the yeast and sugar and add this to the flour.
3. Cover the bowl with a tea-towel and set aside for about 15 minutes.
4. Add the remaining water and salt and combine the ingredients thoroughly.
5. Knead the dough well with the hands or with an electric mixer. Set aside once more for about 30 minutes.
6. Place the dough in a loaf tin, brush the top with lukewarm milk or water and sprinkle a handful of kibbled wheat over the top.
7. Bake for about 50-60 minutes in a pre-heated oven at 400°F/200°C (Gas Mark 6). Place a cupful of water in the oven with the bread.

Bran Rolls

Makes 15-20 rolls

Imperial (Metric)

14 oz (400g) wholemeal flour
5-6 tablespoonsful wheat bran
⅓ pint (200ml) warm buttermilk
1½ oz (40g) dried yeast
1 teaspoonful raw cane sugar
2 teaspoonsful sea salt
3 tablespoonsful vegetable oil
A little aniseed
Bran to coat the rolls

1. Mix together the flour and bran in a bowl and make a well in the centre.
2. Mix a little of the buttermilk with the yeast and sugar, add this to the flour and set aside for 15 minutes.
3. Add the remaining buttermilk, the salt, oil and aniseed, combine the ingredients thoroughly and knead well.
4. Shape the dough into rolls and set them aside again for about 20-30 minutes.
5. Brush the rolls with lukewarm water and sprinkle a little bran over the top.
6. Bake for about 30-40 minutes in a pre-heated oven at 400°F/200°C (Gas Mark 6). These small rolls may be stored in the freezer.

Granary Rolls with Poppy Seeds

Imperial (Metric)

¾ lb (350g) wholemeal flour
6 oz (150g) kibbled wheat
½ pint (¼ litre) lukewarm milk
1½ oz (40g) dried yeast
1 teaspoonful raw cane sugar
1-2 teaspoonsful sea salt
2 oz (50g) polyunsaturated margarine
Lukewarm milk to glaze
Poppy seeds

1. Mix together the flour and kibbled wheat in a bowl and make a well in the centre.
2. Mix a little of the warm milk with the yeast and sugar, add this to the flour and set aside for about 15 minutes.
3. Add the remaining milk with the salt and margarine and combine thoroughly.
4. Knead the dough well and shape it into rolls. Set them aside for 20-30 minutes.
5. Make a small slit in the top of each roll, brush with milk and sprinkle poppy seeds over the top.
6. Bake for about 30 minutes in a pre-heated oven at 400°F/200°C (Gas Mark 6). These rolls may also be stored in the freezer.

Variation
Caraway, sesame seeds or rolled oats may be sprinkled on the rolls instead of poppy seeds.

Quark and Oil Savoury Pastry

Imperial (Metric)

6 oz (150g) Quark
2-3 tablespoonsful milk
2 tablespoonsful vegetable oil
1 teaspoonful sea salt
Pinch of raw cane sugar
1 egg
10 oz (300g) wholemeal flour
¾ oz (20g) baking powder

1. Mix together the Quark, milk, oil, salt, sugar and the egg until smooth.
2. Stir in the flour and baking powder and continue to work with the hands until a supple dough is formed. Set aside for an hour in the fridge.
3. Roll out the dough and cover a large greased baking sheet. (If lining a flan dish, halve the dough; the other half may be kept, well wrapped, for 2-3 days in the fridge.)

Note: If liked, savoury pastries may be made with poppy, caraway, sesame seeds or paprika.

Sweet Quark and Oil Pastry

Imperial (Metric)

6 oz (150g) Quark
2-3 tablespoonsful milk
3-4 tablespoonsful vegetable oil
2 oz (50g) raw cane sugar
1 egg
10 oz (300g) wholemeal flour
¾ oz (20g) baking powder

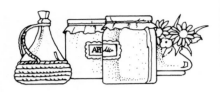

1. Mix together the Quark, milk, oil, sugar and egg until smooth.
2. Stir in the flour and baking powder and knead the dough until soft.
3. Set aside in the refrigerator for 1 hour.
4. Roll out the dough and use it to line a large square baking sheet.
5. Use the dough according to the recipes which require it.

Note: This dough is particularly suitable for fruit cakes and biscuits.

Yeast Pastry

Imperial (Metric)

¾ lb (350g) wholemeal flour
Approx. 4 oz (100g) kibbled wheat
1½ oz (40g) dried yeast
⅓ pint (200ml) lukewarm milk
2 oz (50g) raw cane sugar
2 oz (50g) polyunsaturated margarine or vegetable oil
1 egg
Pinch of sea salt

1. Mix together the flour and kibbled wheat in a warmed bowl and make a well in the centre.
2. Mix the yeast with a little milk and some of the sugar and add this to the flour. Cover with a clean tea-towel and set aside for about 15 minutes in a warm, draught-free spot.
3. Add the remaining milk and sugar, the salt, fat and egg and combine thoroughly with the hands or an electric mixer until the dough leaves the sides of the bowl.
4. Set aside for a further 30 minutes in a warm place until the dough has doubled in size.
5. Knead again and set it aside, either rolled out on a greased baking sheet or in a greased baking tin. Continue according to the recipe used.

Spinach Pizza

Imperial (Metric)

Quark and Oil Savoury Pastry (page 137)
10 tomatoes
Sea salt and freshly ground black pepper
Pinch each of basil, marjoram, garlic salt and nutmeg
4 lb (2 kilos) spinach
7 oz (200g) grated cheese

1. Roll out the pastry and line a greased baking sheet.
2. Wash and slice the tomatoes and place them on the pastry. Season with the salt, pepper, basil and marjoram.
3. Blanch the spinach in a little water and season with the salt, garlic powder and nutmeg.
4. Drain the spinach and spread it over the tomatoes.
5. Top with cheese and bake for about 40 minutes in a pre-heated oven at 400°F/200°C (Gas Mark 6).

Onion Flan

Imperial (Metric)

Half quantity of the Quark and Oil Savoury pastry (page 137)
1¾ lb (¾ kilo) onions, finely sliced
1 tablespoonful vegetable oil
1 small carton natural yogurt
2 eggs
Pinch of raw cane sugar
1 teaspoonful ground caraway seeds
Pinch of ground juniper berries
Sea salt and freshly ground black and white pepper

1. Roll out the dough and line a greased pastry dish.
2. Sauté the onions in the oil and cook for 5-10 minutes over a low heat.
3. Drain the oil out of the onions and arrange them on the dough.
4. Whisk together the yogurt and eggs and season to taste with the remaining ingredients. Spoon the mixture evenly over the onions.
5. Bake for 30-40 minutes in a pre-heated oven at 425°F/220°C (Gas Mark 7).

Note: This should be eaten hot and is particularly good served with a young wine, apple or grape juice.

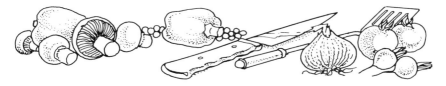

Nut and Carrot Cake

Imperial (Metric)

4 oz (100g) honey
5 eggs, separated
1-2 tablespoonsful Kirsch
10 oz (300g) carrots, finely grated
7 oz (200g) hazelnuts, freshly ground
3 oz (75g) wholemeal flour
Juice of 1 lemon
5 oz (125g) whipped cream to decorate (optional)

1. Beat together the honey and egg yolks until light and frothy and then add the Kirsch.
2. Mix in the carrots and hazelnuts alternately and gradually add the flour. (If the nuts are not finely ground the cake will crumble.)
3. Fold the stiffly beaten egg whites with a spoon and place the mixture in a greased cake tin.
4. Bake in a pre-heated oven for about 40 minutes at 350°F/180°C (Gas Mark 4).
5. Set the cake aside to cool, then make deep holes in the top with a fork. Slowly pour the lemon juice over the top. (If liked, decorate with the whipped cream.)

Baking with Nuts and Dried Fruits

Fruit Loaf

Makes 18-20 pieces   P 5g, F 8g, C 23g, Cals 200

Imperial (Metric)

4 eggs
6-7 tablespoonsful honey
A few drops of pure vanilla essence
1 teaspoonful cinnamon
Pinch of ground cloves
3 oz (75g) almond flakes
6-7 oz (150-200g) hazelnuts
6 oz (150g) raisins
6 oz (150g) dried figs
4 oz (100g) lemon peel, finely diced
6 oz (150g) wholemeal flour
1 heaped teaspoonful baking powder

1. Beat together the eggs, honey, vanilla and spices until creamy.
2. Sprinkle a little flour over the nuts and fruit and add them to the mixture.
3. Combine the flour and baking powder and stir it into the mixture.
4. Spoon the cake mixture into a greased tin and bake for approximately 1½ hours at 350°F/180°C (Gas Mark 4).

Apricot Roll

Makes 25 pieces   P 3g, F 6g, C 25g, Cals 185

Imperial (Metric)

1 lb (½ kilo) wholemeal flour
2 teaspoonsful dried yeast
⅓-½ pint (200-250ml) lukewarm milk
2 oz (50g) honey
Pinch of sea salt
2 oz (50g) vegetable margarine
1 egg

Filling:
¾ lb (350g) dried apricots, soaked for at least 2 hours
Approx. 2 oz (50g) currants
4 oz (100g) flaked almonds
½ teaspoonful ground cloves
Approx. 5 tablespoonsful hazelnut purée
1 egg, separated

1. Combine the flour and yeast in a bowl, then mix in the milk, honey, salt, margarine and egg, either with a mixer or by hand.
2. Set the mixture aside in a warm place for 30-40 minutes, then roll it out to form a square and set aside again for a further 15 minutes.
3. Meanwhile, chop up the well drained apricots and mix in the currants, almonds and cloves.
4. Spread the dough with the hazelnut purée and brush the edges with egg white.
5. Spread the apricot mixture on the pastry dough and roll it up from corner to corner.
6. Set the roll on a greased baking sheet, brush with egg yolk and bake for 40-50 minutes at 400°F/200°C (Gas Mark 6).

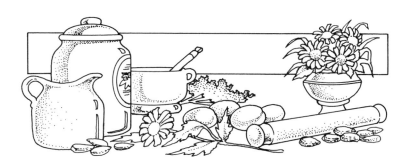

Banana Cake

Makes 20 pieces   P 2g, F 6g, C 21g, Cals 170

Imperial (Metric)

½ lb (¼ kilo) dried bananas
3-4 oz (75-100g) vegetable margarine
2 oz (50g) honey
2 eggs
Few drops of pure vanilla essence
Pinch of nutmeg
Pinch of sea salt
7 oz (200g) wholemeal flour
2 teaspoonsful baking powder
Approx. 4 tablespoonsful milk
2 oz (50g) raisins
2 oz (50g) almonds and coarsely chopped walnuts

1. Soak the bananas in water for about 2 hours.
2. Beat the margarine and honey until creamy, then add the eggs, vanilla, nutmeg, salt, flour and baking powder with a little milk if necessary.
3. Drain the bananas and chop them up, then stir them in with the raisins and nuts to the cake mixture.
4. Spoon the mixture into a greased cake tin and bake for 40 minutes at first at 400°F/200°C (Gas Mark 6) and then after 10 minutes at 350°F/180°C (Gas Mark 4).

Spice Biscuits

Makes about 80   P 1g, F 3g, C 4g, Cals 42

Imperial (Metric)

5 oz (125g) butter
5 oz (125g) raw cane sugar
2 eggs
A little mace, cinnamon, ground cloves and lemon peel
5 oz (125g) wholemeal flour
5 oz (125g) finely ground almonds
5 oz (125g) sesame seeds or crushed wholemeal biscuits

1. Cream the butter, sugar and egg yolks, then add the spices and lemon peel, the sieved flour, almonds and biscuits or breadcrumbs.
2. Knead the dough briefly, adding a little milk if necessary, and roll it out to approximately ¼ inch (½cm) thickness.
3. Cut out biscuit shapes, brush each one with egg yolk and press two almond halves into each one.
4. Bake on an ungreased baking sheet for 10-15 minutes at 350°F/180°C (Gas Mark 4).

Wholemeal Macaroons

Makes approximately 50   P 1g, F 2g, C 5g, Cals 44

Imperial (Metric)

5 oz (125g) kibbled wheat
6 oz (150g) raw cane sugar
A little pure vanilla essence
4 oz (100g) chopped almonds
A little lemon juice
2 oz (50g) melted margarine
2 tablespoonsful wheatgerm
2 egg whites
Approx. 50 rice paper pieces

1. Soak the wheat in the milk for approximately 3 hours then strain it well.
2. Mix the wheat with the sugar, vanilla, almonds, lemon juice, margarine and wheatgerm.
3. Stiffly beat the egg whites and fold them into the mixture.
4. Spoon small amounts of the mixture onto the rice paper and bake at 300°F/150°C (Gas Mark 2) for 10-15 minutes.

9.
DRINKS

Cocoa, coffee, fruit concentrates, all types of fruit (fresh, deep frozen or preserved), vegetable juices, grated vegetables, egg yolk, honey, nuts, liqueurs, brandy, rum or maple syrup.

Lemon Milk

Serves 2   P 10g, F 4g, C 20g, Cals 142

Imperial (Metric)

1 pint (½ litre) milk
Juice of 1-2 lemons
1 tablespoonful honey

1. Blend all the ingredients well and serve immediately before the lemon juice and milk separates.

15.   Baking with fruit and nuts

Raspberry Milk

Serves 2   P 10g, F 4g, C 20g, Cals 142

Imperial (Metric)

1 pint (½ litre) milk
6 oz (150g) fresh or frozen raspberries
Juice of 1 lemon
1 tablespoonful raspberry concentrate

1. Blend all the ingredients well and sieve before serving if preferred.

Blackberry Shake

Serves 2   P 10g, F 9g, C 30g, Cals 250

Imperial (Metric)

1 pint (½ litre) milk
4 oz (100g) blackberries
1 tablespoonful raw sugar blackberry jam
Juice of 1 lemon
1 tablespoonful wheatgerm

1. Blend the milk with the fruit, jam and lemon juice.
2. Sprinkle on the wheatgerm just before serving.

Strawberry Shake

Serves 2   P 10g, F 5g, C 19g, Cals 140

Imperial (Metric)

1 pint (½ litre) milk
4 oz (100g) fresh or frozen strawberries
1 tablespoonful raw sugar strawberry jam
Juice of ½ lemon

1. Blend all the ingredients well.

16.   Winter drinks

145

Fruit and Nut Shake

Serves 2 P 6g, F 4g, C 15g, Cals 125

Imperial (Metric)

1 tablespoonful nut paste
½ pint (¼ litre) pure blackcurrant juice
½ pint (¼ litre) milk
A little honey if liked

1. Blend the nut paste and the fruit juice.
2. Add the milk immediately and stir in honey to taste.

Warming Winter Drinks — Alcohol-Free

Herbal Grog

Serves 4 P 0g, F 0g, C 5g, Cals 20

Imperial (Metric)

1½ pints (¾ litre) thyme tea
½ pint (¼ litre) balm-mint tea
3-4 tablespoonsful maple syrup
A little lemon juice

1. Mix the tea with the maple syrup and lemon juice to taste.

Aniseed and Cinnamon Punch

Serves 4 P 0g, F 0g, C 5g, Cals 20

Imperial (Metric)

5-6 tablespoonsful apple concentrate
2 pints (1 litre) water
1 stick cinnamon
2 stars anise
3 cloves
Juice of 3 lemons
A little lemon rind

1. Mix the apple concentrate with the water and bring to the boil.
2. Add the cinnamon, anise and cloves and leave to stand.
3. Add the lemon juice and rind and serve with a little honey if liked.

Orange-Tea Punch

Serves 4   P 0g, F 0g, C 8g, Cals 30

Imperial (Metric)

2-3 oranges
Juice of 2 lemons
4 teaspoonsful tea
5-7 teaspoonsful honey

1. Wash the oranges well, peel them thinly and press out the juice.
2. Mix the orange juice and peel with the lemon juice and leave for 2-3 hours.
3. Make up approx. 2 pints (1 litre) of fairly weak tea and mix in the fruit juice and honey.

Milk and Pear Punch

Serves 4   P 7g, F 7g, C 22g, Cals 190

Imperial (Metric)

4 pears, halved and cored
2-3 tablespoonsful honey
Juice of 2-3 lemons
Approx. 2 pints (1 litre) milk
Pinch of cinnamon

1. Make a purée of the pears and mix in the honey and lemon juice.
2. Bring the milk to the boil and add to the pear mixture.
3. Pour the punch into warmed glasses and serve with a sprinkling of cinnamon.

Nutritional Table

	Protein g	Fat g	Carbo-hydrate g	Cals	Joules
1 cupful whole milk	4.5	4.5	6.5	85	340
1 cupful skimmed milk	6	2	7	68	272
1 small glass fruit juice	1		12	60	240
1 carton natural yogurt (6 oz/150g)	7		7	60	240
2 tablespoonsful natural yogurt	2	2	2	15	60
1 egg (whole)	7	6		74	296
1 egg yolk	3	6		50	200
1 portion Quark (3-4 oz/80g)	14	4	2	62	248
2 tablespoonsful grated cheese	5	5		70	280
1 oz (25g) vegetable margarine		20		190	760
1 slice wholemeal bread	1		16-18	85	340
1 wholemeal crispbread	1		6	35	140
1 slice wholemeal toast	2		12	70	280
1 piece of cake (2 oz/50g)	3	12	20	200	800
1 piece of diabetic cake (2 oz/50g)	5	10	23	228	912
2 tablespoonsful rolled oats	1.5	3	24	120	480
2 tablespoonsful millet flakes	1.5		12	50	200
1 teaspoonful wheatgerm	1	1	3	25	100
1 teaspoonful yeast flakes	2		1	18	72
1 tablespoonful skimmed milk powder	7		7	55	220
1 teaspoonful raw cane sugar			5	20	80
1 tablespoonful honey			8	30	120
1 tablespoonful vegetable oil		10		92	368
1 tablespoonful mayonnaise		12		114	456
1 tablespoonful milk	1		1	8	32
1 tablespoonful chopped nuts	2	9	2	103	412
6 oz (150g) potatoes	3		30	127	504
6 oz (150g) brown rice	3.5	1	36	185	740
2 oz (50g) millet	6	2	32	182	728
1 cupful soup	2		12	75	300
4 oz (100g) raw vegetable or mixed salad	1		3	20	80
6 oz (150g) green salad	0.5		1	5	20
1 small apple	0.5		12	50	200
1 small orange	1		12	52	204
7 oz (200g) cooked vegetables	4		12	62	248
1 large glass white wine				85	340
1 glass beer				156	624
1 glass diabetic beer			3	103	412
1 whisky				55	220
1 cognac				50	200

INDEX

Aniseed and Cinnamon Punch, 146
Apple Fool, 129
Apple Meringue, 132
Apple Punch, 148
Apple Salad, Sweet, 130
Apples with Rosehips, Baked, 127
Apricot Roll, 141
Artichokes, 69
Artichokes, Dressed, 39
Asparagus, 68
   with Herb Dressing, 68
Asparagus Salad, 106
Aubergine Omelette, 56
Aubergines, Stuffed, 69
Avocados, Stuffed, 40

Banana Cake, 142
Banana Quark with Cinnamon, 126
Bananas, Baked, 127
Barley Casserole, 48
Barley Salad, 112
Barley Soup, Simple, 34
Bean and Red Pepper Savoury, 71

Beetroot Casserole, 48
Beetroot, Savoury, 71
Beetroot with Apples and Horseradish,
   104
Blackberry Shake, 145
Bran Rolls, 136
Broccoli, Sautéed, 72
Broccoli with Cheese, Baked, 73
Broccoli with Hazelnut Butter, 72
Brussels Sprouts in White Sauce, 91
Buckwheat Casserole with Cheese, 64
Buckwheat Porridge, 64
Buckwheat Soup, 33
Buttermilk Soup (Cold), 38

Cabbage Rolls, Soya Stuffed, 74
Cabbage Salad, Sweet, 108
Cabbage, Westfalian, 73
Caraway Potatoes, 94
carbohydrate, 13
Carrot Cakes, 76
Carrot Salad, 105
Carrots, Sautéed, 75

Cauliflower, Baked, 76
Cauliflower with Nuts, 102
Cauliflower with Vinaigrette Dressing, 77
Celeriac Fritters, 78
Celeriac Salad, 104
Celeriac, Savoury, 77
Celery, Baked, 78
Celery, Stuffed, 41
Cheese Omelette, 55
Cheese Salad, 111
Chestnuts, Glazed, 79
Chick Pea Casserole, 49
Chicory au Gratin, 80
Chicory, Indian-style, 79
Chicory with Beetroot and Apples, 102
cholesterol, 153
cold-pressed oils, 12
coltsfoot, 114
Cottage Cheese with Apple, 30
Courgette and Cheese Pasta Omelette, 65
Courgettes in Herby Tomato Sauce, 81
Courgettes, Savoury, 80
Cress Salad, 100
Cucumber Salad, 101
Cucumber Savoury, 82
Cucumber Soup, Greek, 37
Cucumber with Rice Stuffing, 82
Currant Jelly, Mixed, 129

dandelion, 114
Dandelion and Egg Salad, 117
Dandelion Salad, 116
    with Mustard Dressing, 116
Date Quark, 125
dextrose, 14
diabetes, 10, 152
diets,
    Bircher Benner Wholefood, 154
    Fruit, 154
    Juice, 153
    Rice, 154
    Whey, 154
digestive problems, 152
disaccharides, 13

Egg Florentine, 56
Egg Salad, 109
Eggs, Stuffed, 40
Elderberry Soup with Dumplings, 38
Endive Salad, 99
essential nutrients, 10

fat, 12
Fennel and Tomato Savoury, 83
Fennel Salad, 105
Fennel, Sautéed, 83
fibre, 14-15
Frankfurt Dressing, 121
French Bean Casserole, 47
French Beans, 70
Fruit and Nut Shake, 146
Fruit Loaf, 140
Fruit Salad, Mixed, 128
Fruit Salad with Buttermilk, 124
Fruit Soup, Dried, 39

Garlic Dressing (Aioli), 122
Gorgonzola Dressing, 121
Gazpacho, 37
Grain Bread, Mixed, 136
Granary Bread, 135
Granary Rolls with Poppy Seeds, 137
Grape and Banana Salad, 128
Green Pepper Salad, 101
Green Salad, Plain, 99

Hazelnut Quark, 125
Herb Salad, Mixed, 117
Herbal Grog, 146
herbs and spices, 20-22
Honey Custards, 132

Kibbled Wheat Casserole, 60
Kohlrabi, Baked, 84
Kohlrabi, Buttered, 84
Kohlrabi Salad, 106

lactose, 14
Leeks, Baked, 85
Leeks in Cheese Sauce, 85
Lemon Milk, 144
Lentil Casserole, 49
losing weight, 151

Macaroons, Wholemeal, 143
Maize Waffles with Almonds, 63
Milk and Pear Punch, 147
Millet Casserole, 59
Millet Porridge with Apricots, 29
Millet Risotto, 58
Millet Soup, 35
minerals, 16
monosaccharides, 13

Muesli,
    Apple and Banana, 26
    Bran, 27
    Millet Flake, 28
    Quark and Fruit, 27
    Simple Oat, 26
Mushrooms, Sautéed, 86

Nettle Soup, 36
nettles, 114
Nut and Carrot Cake, 140

Onion and Apple Salad, 108
Onion Flan, 139
Onion Soup, 32
Onions, Savoury, 86
Onions, Stuffed, 50
Orange-Tea Punch, 147
Orange Quark, 124

Pancakes, Quark-Filled, 131
Pasta and Mushroom Casserole, 66
Pasta Salad, 110
Pasta Salad with Mushrooms,
    Wholewheat, 110
Peach with Horseradish, Toasted, 42
Pears and Cranberries on Toast, 43
Pears, Stuffed, 41
Peas, Peasant's, 87
Peppered Strawberries, 130
Peppers, Savoury, 88
Polenta, 63
polysaccharides, 14
Porridge, Buckwheat, 29
Porridge with Prunes, 28
Potato and Fennel Casserole, 93
Potato Dumpling, 95
Potato Goulash, 95
Potato Nests, 96
Potato Pancakes with Bran, 96
Potato Soup, 35
Potatoes, Béchamel, 94
Potatoes, Baked, 92
Potatoes with Cream Cheese, 97
protein, 11

Quark and Oil Savoury Pastry, 137
Quark and Potato Casserole, 93
Quark Dumplings, Sweet, 133
Quark Spread, Cheesy, 30
Quark with Peaches, Creamy, 126
Quark with Pears, Creamy, 126

Raspberry Milk, 145
Ratatouille, 70
Red Cabbage Salad with Cheese Dressing,
    109
Red Cabbage, Sweet and Sour, 74
ribwort, 114
Rice — Basic Recipe, 62
Rice Salad, Piquant, 111
Rice Salad with Leeks, 62
Rice-Stuffed Peppers, 87
Rote Grütze, 128

Salad, Mixed, 103
Sauces,
    Caper, 119
    Cheese, 119
    Curry — Mango, 119
    Dill, 119
    Garlic, 119
    Horseradish, 119
    Mushroom, 120
    Mustard, 119
    Paprika, 119
    Tomato, 120
Sauerkraut Casserole, 88
Sauerkraut Salad, Savoury, 89
Sauerkraut Salad, Sweet, 89
Savoy Cabbage, Sautéed, 75
Sesame Waffles, 61
slimming, 153
sorrel, 114
Sorrel Salad, Piquant, 115
Sorrel salad, Sweet, 115
Sorrel Soup, 36
Sour-Dough Starter for Granary Bread, 135
Soya and Aubergine Casserole, 52
Soya and Vegetable Casserole, 51
Soya Bean Sprout Salad, 112
soya beans, sprouting, 54
Soya Dumplings in Tomato Sauce, 53
Soya Goulash, 54
Soya Rissoles with Cheese, 52
Spaghetti with Green Pepper, 66
Spice Biscuits, 142
Spinach and Potato Pudding, 90
Spinach Flan, 90
Spinach Omelette, 57
Spinach Pizza, 139
Spinach Salad, 103
Spinach-Stuffed Tomatoes, 91
Spinach with Egg, Toasted, 43

Spring Soup, 32
storing foods, 17-20
Strawberry Quark, 125
Strawberry Shake, 145
sucrose, 14
Sweetcorn Salad, 109
Sweet Quark and Oil Pastry, 138

Toast, Italian, 44
Tomato Cocktail, 148
Tomato Salad, 100
Tomatoes, Stuffed, 42
Turnip Patties, 92
Turnip Salad, 109

Vegetable Casserole, 47
Vegetable Grapefruit Cocktail, 149
Vegetable Omelette, 55

Vegetable Soup, Italian, 31
    Quick, 33
Vinaigrette Dressing, 122
vitamins, 15-16

watercress, 114
Watercress Salad, 114
Wheat and Leek Soup, 34
Wheat Salad, Sprouted, 113
Wheat Salad with Green Pepper and
    Tomato, 113
White Sauce, Basic, 118
Whole Grains, Basic Recipe for, 58
Wholemeal Dumplings, Sweet, 133
Wholewheat Dumplings, Sweet, 60

Yeast Pastry, 138